University of East Lo

WOMEN AND DIGITAL DIVIDE

WOMEN AND DIGITAL DIVIDE

P Kumar

MD PUBLICATIONS PVT LTD
NEW DELHI
www.mdppl.com

Published by :

MD Publications Pvt Ltd
"MD House", 11, Darya Ganj,
New Delhi - 110 002
Phone : +91-11-45355555
E-mail : contact@mdppl.com
Website: www.mdppl.com

ISBN: 978-81-7533-266-9

Published and Printed by Mr. Pranav Gupta on behalf of **MD Publications Pvt Ltd** at Times Press, Delhi.

PREFACE

The term "digital divide" has traditionally described inequalities in access to computers and the Internet between groups of people based on one or more social or cultural identifiers. Under this conceptualization, researchers tend to compare rates of access to these technologies across individuals or schools based on race, sex, disability status, and other identity dimensions. The "divide" refers to the difference in access rates among groups. The racial digital divide, for example, describes the difference in rates of access to computers and the Internet, at home and school, between those racial groups with high rates of access and those with lower rates of access. Similarly, the sex- or gender digital divide refers to the gap in access rates between men and women.

Ultimately, the traditional understanding of the digital divide as gaps in rates of physical access to computers and the Internet fails to capture the full picture of the divide, its stronghold, and its educational, social, cultural, and economic ramifications. Meanwhile, such a narrow conceptualization of the divide serves the interests of privileged groups who can continue to critique access rates instead of thinking critically and reflectively about their personal and collective roles in cycling and recycling old inequities in a new cyber-form.

Although women use the Internet in greater numbers than men, the number of women who are information technology professionals- producers of information technology rather than simply consumers- lags far behind that of men. Women still comprise less than a quarter of information technology professionals, only eight percent of information technology engineers, and no more than five percent of information technology management. The percentage of women earning degrees in computer science has declined steadily since 1984 and the attrition rate among women computer science students is higher than among men. In particular, minority women make up not more than two percent of information technology professionals in the United States. Furthermore, research has indicated that these percentages will decline.

The gender disparity in interest to learn about information technology is already firmly entrenched at the undergraduate level. According to the Department of Commerce, only 1.1 percent of undergraduate women select information technology disciplines as compared to 3.3 percent of male undergraduates in 1998, and the percentage of women earning bachelor's degrees in information technology fields has dropped steadily since 1984.

I am very grateful to Mr. Pranav Gupta, Director of MD Publications Pvt Ltd, New Delhi, for his kind cooperation and support for this book.

P Kumar

CONTENTS

1

Women and Digital Divide
An Introduction

The word seems to be coming down from Washington these days that it's time to declare victory in the war on the Digital Divide and find new targets for our public policy discussions and interventions. The folks who are saying this are looking at statistics in this country, the United States, that are showing that well over half of all households have access to the Internet, that the proportion of minorities and low-income people who have access to the Internet is increasing overall, and that the cost of Internet access including the cost of the computer to enable the access seems to have come down to a level affordable by most. Parallel developments in many other parts of the world are likely.

Also in the United States, a rising proportion of minority and lower-income populations using the Internet have relieved some of the early anxiety that existing social inequalities would be aggravated in this new and rapidly expanding sphere. Public authorities are being urged to relax and let the market continue what appears to be the inexorable drive to more or less universal Internet access (with all those wanting access having access). This argument leads to an emerging position that there is no need to fund development of local technology projects or for public Internet access through community technology centers, which in other countries would be called telecenters, telekiosks, telepublicos, and so on.

The broad public discussion and policy commitment in support of the public use of information and communications technologies (ICTs) seems to have stalled, and we are being urged to turn our attention to other things, with Internet access for shopping and sending the occasional e-mail to one's friends and family now so widely accessible. However, the realism of these observations, how this position seems to exclude the 30 or 40 per cent of the population even in the United States, still without Internet access, let alone the tens of millions in developing countries who don't even have electricity or telephone, let alone Internet access, is not the focus of this chapter.

The use of the Internet is quietly and inexorably triggering a "digital revolution" throughout the entire United States economy and among leading elements of the global economy. The transformations brought about by introducing digital systems and the Internet enabled business operations to be as profound, sweeping, and disruptive as anything that was achieved in the heady days of the early Industrial Revolution.

Digital technologies are with accelerating force and speed introducing new operating efficiencies, service delivery opportunities, and market response flexibilities, as well as an unprecedented access to customers and suppliers that is reshaping the competitive structures of whole industries virtually overnight. The result can be seen in rapid run-ups in market concentration and dramatic rises (and falls) in market capitalization. Dramatic changes are taking place in supply chains, customer relationship systems, and value networks with suppliers and strategic partners. As one example, a generation ago, a pharmacist in a small Canadian town would fill perhaps 8,000 prescriptions a year. Today, Merck-Medco the pharmaceutical giant has developed a Web-enabled dispensary where 8,000 prescriptions an hour, having been entered through a Web site, are being robotically dispensed without human intervention.

Accompanying this are startling reallocations of social position and wealth, unexpected changes in local, regional, and even national labour markets, and accelerated concentrations of political, economic, cultural, and social influence. All of this in turn is masking a deep and fundamental shift in opportunities and life chances for many intranationally and internationally as the demand for skills and experience and local resources evolve rapidly in response.

As a comparison, one might look to the types of changes that occurred during the Industrial Revolution, many of which became visible in their scope and significance only generations later. The productive benefits that are currently being brought about in efficiency, productivity, speed of response, scope, and breadth of market influence are accessible only to those with the resources and the quite considerable knowledge required to take advantage of these opportunities.

Primarily the corporate sector, and only certain elements within the corporate sector, has been in a position to take advantage of the revolutionary potential presented by ICTs. Others, those without such access the not for profits, the local public sector, those outside the market and beyond the enabling technology networks seem to be falling ever further behind. These organizational groups have been left without support. Where there has been attention at all, that attention has been couched in efforts to bridge the digital divide for Internet access. This approach makes the bold assumption that simply achieving access was a substitute for acquiring the means of making effective use of the technology.

The attention of the technology designers and implementers-the hardware and software developers, the consultants and the venture capitalists has been focused ever more intensively on the corporate sector and on the commercial and corporate applications of ICTs. Other uses such as those by lower-income communities, the marginalized, and the small and microbusinesses are being left largely unattended.

What has not been done, and why the declaration of victory by those concerned with the public good is shortsighted and ultimately destructive, is that the opportunities for providing public goods using the same digital technologies, opportunities for enabling and supporting the creation and recreation of caring communities, has only barely been recognized. Instead we see only experiments and pilot projects in online support groups for seniors, in providing information systems to tertiary caregivers, in training and public access centers for those with financial or other constraints to achieving individual access. But, as the money for experiments runs out and the volunteers lose their steam, the projects disappear and the Internet is left as a marketplace for those with the resources and access to support use in this growing technology.

Every reputable university in this country and probably in almost every country in the world has a faculty teaching and researching management information systems (MIS). However, not one department anywhere in the world at the moment is known to be devoted to community information systems to research, teaching, or development to support parallel development processes for those working to enable communities to use information systems effectively.

The world is being transformed with ICTs. The early promise, however, of the Internet as an alternative to centralized concentrations of power and wealth and as a means for widely dispersing economic opportunity has faded to be replaced first by the DotCom bubble and then by the current drive to make the Internet an adjunct to cyberspace shopping malls. The early vision of the Internet as an enabler of communities; of the isolated; the disabled; those excluded because of location, income or physical capacity; seems to have disappeared along with public efforts supporting the Internet as a tool and a resource for all, a democratizer and an equalizer.

GLOBALIZATION AND LOCAL COMMUNITIES

While communities are becoming ever more subject to external forces over which they have little or no control, ICTs present significant opportunities and even advantages to local communities. At the least, they reduce barriers of distance and location, while supporting local communities as they attempt remote or distributed self-management. Decentralized computing linked to a communications capacity allows for work to be done from any networked remote location. This can be used to access skills and training, to level the playing field for technology-oriented education and training, to decentralize information-intensive public sector activities, and as a way of equalizing employment opportunities between rural and urban areas.

ICTs present the opportunity for

- Local ownership and management of local information
- Participation in information-intensive activities at a distance
- Introduction of local priorities into the processing of information to take advantage of economies of disaggregation
- Synergies of distributed production networks
- The flexibility of small-scale distributed management and control

For small communities, ICTs can mean access to markets and suppliers, to information providers, and to others for mutual support and the possibility of competing effectively if remotely with globalized producers.

Local groups can emerge, inspired by the activities of others in distant places but with common concerns and common goals. Information can be shared seamlessly back and forth and in individual locales. Local concerns and local resources can supplement and complement the broader frameworks and add strength both through numbers and through technical and other subject-specific contributions to the overall project.

COMMUNITY INFORMATICS AND COMMUNITY NETWORKS

Community informatics (CI) is the application of information and communications technologies (ICTs) to enable community processes and the achievement of community objectives including overcoming digital divides both within and among communities. But CI also goes beyond discussions of the digital divide. It goes on to examine how and under what conditions ICT access can be made usable and useful to the range of excluded populations and communities and particularly to support local economic development, social justice, and political empowerment using the Internet.

Thus a framework is emerging for systematically approaching information systems from a community perspective that parallels MIS in the development of strategies and techniques for managing community use and application of information systems closely linking with the variety of community networking research and applications. This is based on the assumption that geographically based communities (also known as physical or geo-local communities) have characteristics, requirements, and opportunities that require different strategies for ICT intervention and development from the widely accepted implied models of individual or in-home computer/Internet access and use. Because of cost factors, much of the world is unlikely to have in-home Internet access in the near future.

Thus CI represents an area of interest both to ICT practitioners and academic researchers and to all those with an interest in community-based information technologies addressing the connections between the academic theory and research, and the policy and pragmatic issues arising from community networks, community technology centers, telecenters, community communications centers, and telecottages currently in place globally.

What characterizes this approach to public computing is

- A commitment to universality of technology-enabled opportunity including to the disadvantaged.
- A recognition that the "lived physical community" is at the very center of individual and family well-being-economic, political, and cultural.
- A belief that this can be enhanced through the judicious use of ICTs.
- A sophisticated user-focused understanding of Information technology.
- Applied social leadership, entrepreneurship, and creativity.
- Networked linkages (particularly ethnic or cultural) in urban communities as compared to the more limited overlapping

in rural communities.

This includes the ongoing economic or institutional sustainability of local access and questions on how community informatics approaches will survive once initial funding sources and volunteer participation are exhausted. This in turn raises issues of the ongoing benefits of ICTs to local communities. A theory and a practice of community informatics is thus gradually developing.

This is arising partly out of experiences with community access and community networks in the United States and Canada and partly out of a need to develop systematic approaches to some of the challenges which ICTs are surfacing with astonishing speed. This includes the recognition that access in itself is insufficient; rather, it is what is and can be done with the access that makes ICTs meaningful and a recognition that there is a need to ensure a local, civic, and public presence in an increasingly commercialized Internet environment.

Equally, the use of ICTs as a basis for local economic development and as a way to enable and support local innovation is of considerable interest. Of particular interest does the context of communities have to adjust to the often dramatic changes in local circumstances and opportunities resulting from technology change and globalization of production and competition? Meanwhile, ICTs are emerging as a tool for enabling the development and enhancing the effectiveness of local leadership. They are providing the means to create collaborative networks of economic, social, and political initiatives particularly for local responses to externally imposed change.

The development of strategies to enable management use of ICTs to accomplish corporate ends is a well-recognized and widely supported component of business research, education, and training. Community informatics provides a parallel set of opportunities for those interested in enabling community objectives with ICTs. Community networks and community networking are ways to develop and control locally based information systems to support local development, even though those local processes oppose or even directly conflict with globalized and remotely managed technology and economic activities.

Where MIS empowers and enables managers and particularly corporate managers to extend the power and practice of increasingly globalized corporate structures, community networking and CI are looking to enable local communities developing the means and the capacity to counter the typically hierarchical processes of large-scale organizations. In this, community networking and CI are using technology systems and particularly networking capacity to support the management of local activities and to create mutually supportive networks of efforts whose functioning distributes control rather than centralizing it.

When addressing the first Global Communities Networks Congress in Barcelona in 1999, Manuel Castells saw this approach to community networking as a basis of opposition to globalization by enabling community processes. This approach also develops the pragmatics and the theories to extend the variety of enabled community processes-community development, e-health, e-culture, e-government and e-politics, and not least e-exchange and e-commerce.

A variety of new applications develop as computing facilities are made available in communities. Locally based enterprises begin to use the Internet to promote and advertise their products. Local destinations present themselves on the Internet as destinations that include the opportunity to link to or make reservations at local hotels and bed and breakfasts, local entertainment facilities, and others such as local campgrounds, or to make reservations to visit local artists or artisans. Other communities use the opportunity to take possession (and ownership) of its own "memories" or history and particularly the outputs of its own culture and language.

As the larger forces of globalization are increasingly working to incorporate more and more local production and locally based culture and knowledge within their marketing frames or as intellectual property protected by rules of copyright and patent, communities in turn can use the technologies to preserve, capture, and exert ownership over the results of local cultural development, production, history, and knowledge. An area of particular interest and potential long-term importance for local and community empowerment is community telehealth/telemedicine.

Health resources are increasingly being made available on the Internet often through commercial and sometimes questionable sources. Internet users are increasingly migrating to the Internet as sources of health-related information and as "second opinions" concerning professional medical advice. Having access to Internet-based information and Internet-delivered medical or health services will significantly enhance the health care available locally in remote or underserved areas and support the development of local processes of health care management.

However, the key challenge is to ensure that the information available is both reliable and appropriate for local requirements. Thus there is a need not only for general (globally oriented) health information, but also for information of more specifically local or regional interest, in that medical conditions and facilities vary dramatically from locale to locale and information that may be pertinent to those accessing it in a very well serviced United States suburb may not be as useful or appropriate for those living in remote regions of Appalachia or Senegal, for example.

Through the combination of remote service and support, and local management and delivery, local health care can be improved and individuals can develop increased responsibility for managing their and their communities' health. Similarly, user-friendly interfaces and ever more sophisticated database management software are allowing geographic information systems (GIS) displaying and processing data in graphic and map-based forms to play an ever more significant role in supporting communities to exert democratic control over local physical and socioeconomic resources.

The development of innovative approaches to user interfaces for GIS data and for linking GIS data into decision support systems for policy analysis and advocacy is allowing even the least literate citizens can understand and begin to act upon patterns of resource distribution (and maldistribution), environmental issues, matters of health epidemiology, and so on.

Finally, there is an ever increasingly close linkage between communities and those with highly developed technical skills and a social activist perspective, have been involved in the Free Software Movement and Open Source developments such as Linux. The significance of Free Software, Shareware, or Open Source software for community technology initiatives is in part that many community initiatives use these software platforms and products because of cost and to a degree because of a belief that there is a shared set of broader antimonopolist social values.

The formation of online networks for distributed social, economic, and political organization and development presents communities with a significant new opportunity. The technology allows for instantaneous and continuous communication, work sharing, and remote administration and management. The possibility of creating multinodal networks of local communities coordinated by technology which present themselves as single units to the outside world is only beginning to be explored.

The advantage of this through the creation of economies (and aggregations) of scale for procurement, sales, and marketing and for service contracting (similar in some respects to earlier face-to-face-based producer and consumer cooperatives) while evident to many requires a relatively high degree of technical sophistication and social entrepreneurship. However, this direction presents significant opportunities for scaling local technology initiatives (as, for example, community technology centers) that in many cases would be a precondition for achieving a significant degree of financial and organizational sustainability.

Flexible networking emphasizes coordination of production or distribution based on optimization of selective advantages within the network and the use of the larger-scale capacities of the network to undertake more elaborate activities. Both of these lend themselves to application in the variety of areas of community enablement through ICT including e-health and e-culture.

A major source of opportunity and strength is thus available for small local communities. Previous limitations based on small and dispersed population, limited available of skills, and little opportunity to obtain the advantages that arise from specialization could now be overcome through using technology as substitute for population propinquity. A flexible network could draw on the advantages both of specific geographic locales and from the economies and efficiencies of scale as a component of a larger network of local and independent actors in competing for markets or as a basis for putting together project teams for contractual servicing or production.

A virtual (electronic network thus could for practical purposes function as a virtual enterprise or an extended networked virtual city including a number of smaller localities interacting and coordinating with each other through horizontal electronic communications. Such extended electronic localities could take advantage of the very real changes in the operational functionalities that the technology affords. These include allowing for the locale to function so as to optimize the advantages of ICTs including the lower cost structure and flexibility of response of distributed locations.

Successful projects share a common strategy. They expand the resources and information available locally by collaborating through personal and technology networks with related efforts in other communities and elsewhere at the regional or international level. These new types of networked organizations are structured as hubs and multiple self-sufficient nodes with collaborative specializations, information dispersal, and multiple or distributed information creation and ownership. They have decentralized and horizontal support structures, and a high degree of local self-sufficiency.

With this, of course, goes a speed of adaptation and of information flow horizontally rather than vertically, and economies of mutual peer support rather than functional support. Add to this the opportunity to adapt responses closer to the precipitating events both geographically and culturally, and this can be highly competitive in larger, even global, contexts as networks must respond to rapidly changing conditions that are both local and global and adapt their responses both to local requirements and to evolving global frameworks.

It should be clear that would is emerging through the creation of dispersed and flexible localized networks is a new form of networked community power where power is available in distributed nodes, linked electronically and capable of working in concentrated, cohesive, and coordinated fashion when responding to larger-scale issues as well as focusing dispersed network resources to the resolution of issues and activities of local concern. In this we can see the development of new and local foci of power which are not necessarily structured in relation to centralized systems of (for example, state) power. In this way can be seen an opportunity for developing locally based yet internationally linked structures and organizations which can act as a counterforce to the centralizing and globalizing forces of neoliberalism.

All of this, of course, would be mapping onto the strengths and resiliency of existing communities while enabling highly adaptive responses to rapidly evolving external economic and other conditions. Local communities are also assisted in evolving toward increasing information intensity, increasing sophistication in their response to local and external markets, increasing local complexity and product specialization, increasing capacity for dispersed coalition building, and being able to integrate or evolve directly into dispersed decision-making structures. The resulting disintermediation and blurring of organizational boundaries between user and supplier, citizen and the state, are precisely what many predict will be the organizational model responding to an Internet-enabled economy and polity of the immediate future.

Certainly there is no inevitability of locally based ICTs leading to locally based development. In many respects, ICTs centralize and delocalize developments as much as they enable them. On the one hand the Internet and IT overall promote the free flow of capital, employment, and information with the effect that they shift toward where they can obtain the highest and most immediate returns. However, ICTs present to local communities access to unprecedented quantity and quality of resources-information, skills and markets.

The challenge is to find the means to realize the potentials that ICTs provide even while they competition and the pace of change quicken and intensify. For those who are prepared to accept the challenge an individual looking for a local livelihood in a home town, a community searching for a strategy of survival as its traditional economic base declines, a region or a country looking to refocus its energies toward the modern and the growing-ICTs can be the source of hope and direction.

To date, the vision of the information society has largely been that of the "winners"-those for whom the opportunities for technology, business, or even social innovation presented by ICTs have struck an immediate and productive chord. Enormous creative and productive energies have been let loose by the Internet and information technology even including the financial (but not technology) bubble of the DotComs. But the technology also opens up enormous opportunity for others because of its plasticity; its capacity to make available at low or marginal cost enormously valuable resources of information, communications, and digital manipulation; its ability to rearrange settle hierarchies of location-focused privilege and power.

Indeed it might be said that many of those applications that could be of greatest social (and economic or distributional) benefit have been left largely unexplored and undeveloped in the wake of the DotCom gold rush and the current drive to re-create the Internet as a commercial plow-horse. The absence of funds or attention to social and social organizational experimentation and development with the Internet will surely be seen as one of the more seriously misdirecting impacts of the current market ascendancy.

The microcomputer's promise toward decentralization, dispersal and extension of access to productive resources and capacities (information as a productive resource only develops as with other resources alongside enabling policy, financial and commercial infrastructures). The very real potential for local (and individual) empowerment arising from the PC (personal computer) revolution can be realized only if other resource elements of production are similarly repositioned to support this.

Even as the local is falling behind in the face of current technologies, we have the prospect of a continuing tidal wave of further technologies. Almost in place, for example, is the availability of virtually unlimited bandwidth and thus interactive as well as one-way communications capability with Broadband either through fixed fiber optic cable or via satellite or increasingly, at least for the final from the network connection, through wireless.

Even the commercial implementers of these systems are unsure as to what applications may be most desirable to the consumers, not to speak of the development of community-enhancing applications, although, some of those who are most creatively propelling fixed wireless "last mile" solutions for Broadband seem to see communities as possible owners or maintainers of this component of the network with some very interesting possibilities for the development of locally enhancing applications and social relations.

All of these increased communications powers thus present both risks and opportunities for local communities. The challenge is to find ways to realize these opportunities, when there is so little support or even vision of how these technologies could enable communities, enhance local developments, and empower local citizens in the face of on-rushing global forces with seemingly unlimited wealth and the capacity to influence all sectors and not incidentally finding ready allies within state structures at both the political and the bureaucratic levels.

While those who can command huge resources are able to respond and take advantage of the pace and depth of technology changes, in the absence of external financial support, and of aggregations of locally oriented research and particularly development initiatives, the risk that the local will get lost amid the rubble resulting from the changes induced by the global becomes ever more acute.

The opportunities presented by the technologies for enhancing, enabling, and empowering, however, are too great to abandon the terrain-leaving technology as a tool only for the globalizers, the rich, and the powerful. To not move forward to explore and extend the local applications of technology for local ends is to abandon both those who value the local and what is provides and those who have little choice but to seek their futures in the local to a very uncertain social and economic future.

In the end, it will come down to the capacity of citizens to re-exert control over the public good. There is an ever-growing need to ensure that the opportunities presented by ICTs are made as available to enrich the capacities of local communities as they are to enrich the range of consumer choices and corporate efficiencies. This is perhaps the most important public task of the coming decade. Widespread availability of Internet access is only the beginning. Enabling the use of these technologies to achieve local benefits economic, social, cultural, and political to provide foundations for local communities-caring communities and caring services will require the concentrated efforts of technologists, researchers, and community practitioners and overall a political will to develop and implement these applications.

THE DIGITAL DIVIDE IN HIGHER EDUCATION

There is something emerging called "eBlack." It's clear from scholars and popularizers that the concept of the information age or information revolution fits a general understanding of the periodization of history. Looking at history writ large, we can see that there have been at least three revolutions in which technology impacted the economy and other aspects of society: first, the agriclrural revolution, the domestication of plants and animals, the establishment of settled communities and so on; next, the industrial age emerging with the importance of machines, the rapid increase in productivity and quality of life; and, now, this wonderful high-speed information revolution-where we are in its maternity ward.

Many things about the information revolution are perhaps most like the anxious worrying of parents about what's going to happen to their child. We are, in fact, at the beginning, and we are not quite sure what are going to happen. Being at the beginning is why it's important to have a value orientation, as opposed to locking into a particular stage of hardware, software, or any application that might be popular now and that these three revolutions are code words for how one might rethink the history of the African-American experience.

That history does not fit the overall historical sequencing of the three great revolutions, but it does suggest that the actual experience of African Americans has had a similar periodization, in the relationship of both African-American labour to the technological base and organization of the economy and also to cultural and social life. In other words, in thinking about African-American life in the South, one can easily reconceptualize it in terms of technology. For example, the invention of the cotton gin placed great demands for field labour, and, consequently, the rise of the Cotton Kingdom indeed, cotton was king. Not regionalized in the South, cotton was, in fact, the dominant feature of the entire economy.

More wealth was invested in slaves and the production of cotton than all of the entire U.S. economy put together-all banks, all industry, all railroads, everything. The production of cotton internationally dominated the U.S. role in world trade. Thus, it is not a regional phenomenon but a technological development that served as the material basis for the entire country. The end of this does not occur, of course, with the Civil War, a political and social development.

From a technological point of view and from the point of view of labour and what was actually happening in the lives of people in the South, the change occurs in the 1940s with the mechanical cotton picker. From the standpoint of technology and labour, the movement from slavery to sharecropping shows great consistency with some change between the social organizations of labour in the plantations versus its subsequent deconstruction into sharecropping.

The point is that one can look at African-American history from the standpoint of technology. That enables us to see the emergence of industrialization, the great migrations to the city that happens at precisely the moment when industrial jobs start getting exported out of the city, even though there was a period of overlap. The industrial system in the city was already in decline before blacks arrived. Positions in service and information have risen, surpassing the industrial labour force already declining in the 1950s.

The industrial period for African Americans was not the late nineteenth century but rather toward the middle of the twentieth century. The question we are faced with today is whether or not a similar lag is going to occur with regard to the information revolution. Of course, when we think about the difference between the information society and industrial society, we begin to see important developments.

The important point is that wealth continues to be generated, production continues to go on, and the things we need continue to be available. Then, the question becomes, what do we do with people who don't have to go to work? And how do we figure out how to distribute wealth so that we can ensure a quality of life in this society without turning it into a garrison state? Fundamentally, that's the issue today.

The message is seen in having the crime rate go down while federal policy is increasing the number of police on the streets; schools being closed and prisons being built, not just in California, but also in Toledo, Ohio. We are, in fact, moving more toward the garrison state, toward gated communities. We are moving to a high value for homogeneity even though the society may be diverse in color or language. Fundamentally, what we are talking about is a certain kind of homogeneity that gives us comfort. We have to take the long view and be critical of this because it has serious implications for everybody not inside the gate: They will indeed storm the gate.

THE AFRICAN EXPERIENCE

Clearly, one of the major points about the information society is that it is about the central role of knowledge the production, distribution, consumption, application of knowledge. When we look at the global scene, we see that the continent of Africa has 13 per cent of the world's population but considerably less than that when it comes to the production of knowledge. Africa is starting out considerably behind in the information age.

One indicator is telephones, an indicator relative to the industrial age with wires, telephone poles, cables on the ocean floor, and so on. Something like 90 per cent of the African population has never made a telephone call. There are more phone lines in Manhattan than in all of Africa. On the other hand, what's interesting is that new telephones in Africa are mainly wireless, cellular. In other words, the new information age has technology that enables Africans to skip over one era and create the possibility for communicating in ways that in the next decades will cause a revolution in consciousness.

This is different from highways. With highways, there are unintended consequences like the spread of AIDS with truck drivers and armies. But with telephones, the languages and consciousness of Africa, always guided in the modern era by a unity theme, suddenly get a boost. African nationalism has always meant the unification of Africa. Now, for the first time, there will be a tool, an instrument to enable people-beyond governments, NGOs, and so on to communicate and build in very practical terms this consciousness of unity in order to get around some of the problems that African societies are facing.

What I am asserting is that old inequalities are being reproduced in the first stage of the information revolution. And when it comes to the Internet, it's very clear that we are starting off with "them that's got shall have," the old Billie Holiday song. We are talking about the first stage of the adoption of new technology. In the advanced industrial countries with a high per centage of people who are Internet users in Europe and the U.S., predictions are that in the next ten to twenty years the picture is going to be very different on a global scale.

The current dominance in Internet use by the developed countries is likely to decline dramatically as Asia, Latin America, and Africa begin to adopt information technology and use new telecommunications tools. In urban areas of Ghana, there is a great thirst among the population connected to the university, middle-classes, the government, and NGOs, to use information technology. From a computer lab at the University of Ghana, the contradiction is that as students are trained, where do they go to work? How do they work and live in their communities? It's clear that African leaders are very much focused on this.

Former South African President Mandela identified it as a critical issue. In South Africa, they are using the concept of the telecenter. We're familiar with the cybercafe and community technology centers. This is their equivalent: to bring everything from the telephone, Xerox, fax machines, and access to the Internet. Telecenters are government-sponsored programs designed to have local entrepreneurs, as they're trained, take them over. The South African government has established that 50 per cent of the people who should own these community technology centers and be managers should be women. It's a very progressive development. There is a focus on information technology. Yet, the fact remains that there is a digital divide that reflects the relation of the campus to the community.

Now, moving to our situation, it's interesting that through the Department of Commerce, the government has, over the last four to six years, generated data about the digital divide. Larry Irving, who was the person in charge, developed and popularized the concept of the digital divide. We should be clear that the current buzz-word of "digital opportunity" is now being debated. Digital divide suggests that there is an information-poor side of the polarity. When we say "digital opportunity," we want to keep that term but not to the extent that it makes us forget about the real polarity that exists.

There are at least three fundamental issues we've got to deal with. The term "cyberdemocracy" involves two things: First, it involves access access to the hardware and the software. But it also involves literacy that is, not only functional literacy, the ability to use these and have applications that are useful, but social literacy. Social literacy raises the empowerment question of how to use the technology to serve one's social, political, and cultural ends and not just to fit into a niche that qualifies for this or that particular job.

In other words, cyberdemocracy implies that access and literacy are issues to constantly be worked on. The access part is almost a done deal. It's being driven by the dot-coms and by the transformation of the economy. Literacy is not a done deal. Literacy is the ability to empower people to use this technology outside the occupational niches the economy has constructed. Secondly, there is the concept of "collective intelligence." Now everything from H.G. Well's book *The World Brain*, to the impulse toward encyclopedias, toward indexing, and the impulse toward aggregating knowledge writ large.

At every stage in human history, when a change occurs, there's a desire to encompass everything, to try to get a perspective. At this stage, what we have is a tradition of vertical relationship in the production and distribution the trickling down if you will-of knowledge. In the information age we re talking about the ability to reverse that from vertical to horizontal, fishing with a net, letting all the voices be heard, having the tools to analyze so that the patterns inside all that knowledge are accessible. Thereby, everybody becomes a producer of knowledge, and everybody's voice can be heard.

Lastly, the question of "information freedom." Democracy is always about maximizing an experience for everyone in the society or in the social group. We started out with the promise of the information superhighway being a free highway for everybody. Then the shell game went down, the dust cleared, and we found out we have a railroad and not a superhighway. What do I mean? If you remember how railroads were constructed in this country, millions of acres of land were given to private companies to build what would be a service.

Then, if you wanted to ride or send some goods you had to pay, and that was interpreted as logically correct: Give them what you then have to pay for. Here we have the information age with the Telecommunications Act, which few paid attention to, whereby the fundamental legal and economic relations of the information society were constructed. The issue of information freedom-as opposed to information for sale brings up a public library system. It brings up the role of universities in soc iety which, it seems to me be they public or private is to create a public sphere where everyone in the society can participate in the production and direction not only of cultural values but of policy, of the direction, the basic decisions of what go on in this society.

Now, by way of transitions, it's clear that when we talk about cyberdemocracy and access we have a little history because of the telephone. The telephone is the tool now that is virtually everywhere. If you're in the inner-city and you don't have a phone in your house, there's one some blocks away. It may not always work, but it's there. As I said, access to the equipment is being given, like cell phones given away in order to use. That is very likely to be the case with computers. In other words, the tool itself is not going to be what generates money. It's the use of it. And the question is whether or not the use of it is going to be in the public sphere or entirely in the commodity market.

Our approach to cyberdemocracy and to literacy is that we think the way to look at cyberdemocracy is not to look at it from the standpoint only of the information-rich reaching out to the information-poor. The question is, who do they reach out to? And what is the connection? In other words, if you think about a bridge, it spans something by drilling down and sticking a steel girder in granite, in rock. It has to be done on both sides of the river. So we know what the information-rich side is: government, the institution-driven work, the private sector. But what is it on the other side of the digital divide? What do you hook up with that enables people to get across this chasm?

For what makes democratic society possible, I turn to Robert Putnam's Bowling Alone to ask what it is about communities that produces a high level of participation forming a basis for democracy. His concept of social capital breaks down into two parts: bonding social capital and bridging social capital. Bonding social capital is that capital within a community a church, a neighborhood group, an extended family that shares something and trusts each other. Bridging social capital represents some group or some influence from elsewhere coming in to help.

For example, in the civil rights movement, we see the bridging kinds financial contributions from the North-were important. However, that was not the basis of the civil rights movement; it was the bonding social capital from within the Black community. Bridging was necessary but not sufficient. It's necessary to mobilize the social basis of a community in order to have something sustaining there. A book by a British sociologist, Tim Jordan, develops three kinds of cyberpower. Individual, through skills acquisition and so on. Social cyberpower is the use of information technology to achieve community ends. And ideological cyberpower is the presentation of ideas and the development of consensus and that is what I am talking about in this chapter.

For the first time in history, says Kennedy School Professor Jane Fountain, women have the opportunity to play a major and visible role in a social transformation of "potentially monumental proportions." Of course, Fountain is talking about information technology a field that has virtually seeped into every facet of our lives, from what we drive to where we bank to how we keep in touch. Still, notes Fountain, women may not be able to capitalize on this opportunity if their numbers in information design roles don't expand.

"Traditionally, IT-related fields haven't been as diverse as they need to be. But the question, 'Who designs technology?' matters greatly now that information technology is becoming increasingly pervasive in business, government, and nonprofit sectors. IT has become a critical element in most of the products and services we use. As computing touches more and more areas of our lives, the social implications of design hardware, software, and interfaces become critically important.

"Important streams of research in psychology and management demonstrate that diversity in problem-solving groups leads to different and often better outcomes. The results tend to be more inclusive, that is, they tend to take into consideration the values, interests, and needs of a variety of different parties. Attention to a wider range of computing users would benefit society.

"The gap between the number of women and men getting computer science degrees is actually getting wider, but signs of progress exist for younger students. Beginning in 1997, girls and boys began playing computer games at equal levels in grade nine. Internet use by elementary and middle school children has not differed by gender since 1997. But only 17 per cent of students in AP computer science courses are girls. A number of policy interventions could reduce inequality and transform the construction of an information-based society."

2

The Telecenter Movement

Our correspondent says that you can get to the World Internet Learning Center by driving 100 kilometers north from Harare, Zimbabwe. In Bindura there it is one of thirteen sites selected in the country for the World Bank sponsored World Links for Development model of a dual-use telecenter. It serves students and teachers in the surrounding schools by day and the general community and adult learners during the evenings, weekends, and holidays.

Across the world, tribal leader Oswaldo Rosas could think of few benefits modern life had brought to his people-until a brilliant sunny day when the Internet reached his Ashaninka Indian village in central Peru. The story goes on to tell how, through grants from the Canadian government, the local telephone company, and a nonprofit organization, things were changed by the introduction of a computer, portable generator, satellite dish, and big screen monitor. Rosas and five other tribal leaders received eight weeks of computer training which led to developing their own Ashaninka Web site. With it they sold their organically grown oranges in Lima, 250 miles away, and boosted tribal revenue 10 per cent. Now, Rosas's hut also doubles as a tribal cyber cafe.

These two stories from developing nations reflect some of the changes being offered by the new information and communication technologies (ICTs). It is a dramatic phenomenon, but not without some complications. For example, the benefits of information technologies are reaching the Ashaninkas in Peru, but almost all of the middle-aged women there cannot read or write (a situation common in the poorest Latin American countries).

They are like millions of people all over the world who may be shut out of the information society because of their literacy level, their gender, or their poverty. Most are likely never to open the door of a telecenter or push the start button of a computer. A variety of factors point to the long-term importance of "being connected." One can argue about the costs and benefits of globalization, but not its inevitability or its significance for the dramatic events happening in the cyber world.

And even on a smaller scale, the proliferation of "e" terms such as e-governance, e-commerce, and e-education suggest that getting along even in one's own community may relate to being connected. This reality surfaced in South Africa in late 2001 when the government launched 100 public information terminal systems in rural areas that until then had no access to electronic information. The project, which will give 20 million people access to global information via the Internet, allows people to open an e-mail box and send and receive e-mail. Links to government Web sites provide them with information about regulations, welfare programs, and government activities.

This chapter explores the emergence of community-based organizations in developing countries that provide their populations with connectivity to information technologies. While there are many variations, three forms dominate the world scene.

TELECENTERS

Typically, telecenters offer a broad range of communication services related to the needs of the community, some of which are free or subsidized by external bodies such as governments or NGOs. These might include desktop publishing, community newspapers, sales or rental of audio and videocassette and DVDs, book lending, training, photocopying, faxing, and telephone services. Others, like the Hungarian telecottages and the Western Australia Telecenter Network telecenters, offer other community services such as banking and employment services.

The idea of a community sharing computer technology emerged in the 1980s with the introduction of telecottages in Scandinavia. The initial purpose of those telecottages was to fight against the marginalization of remote rural places in the anticipated information society. With the sprouting of the Internet in the 1990s, a new breed of telecottages appeared in Hungary. Supported initially by the U.S. Agency for International Development (USAID), these telecottages were built around computers, the Internet, and social and economic development.

Oddly, the Hungarian program was less a technology initiative and more an effort to help Hungary build a local government system after the collapse of the centralized political and economic structure. Hungarian telecottages were part of the robust movement that marked the close of the twentieth century, with momentum that has continued into this century: Hungary, for example, is planning to expand its telecottage program from 100 to 500 through 2005.

CYBER CAFES

The commercially oriented cyber cafes that are found from streets adjoining China's Tiananmen Square to the neighborhoods of Buenos Aires are part of an equally robust movement. They are usually in the private sector and focus primarily on providing customers with the use of computers and connections to the Internet and the World Wide Web. Their clients tend to be more urban, more educated, and more economically well off than the clients of telecenters.

By their nature, at this period of the telecenter movement, telecenters tend to be in the public and civil society sector and focus on more isolated people (such as villagers) and those with lower income and low education levels. While both cyber cafes and telecenters might offer training in computer and Web use, the telecenter is more likely to offer other kinds of training, including nonformal education and distance learning in agriculture, health, basic education, entrepreneurship, and other fields particularly related to community development.

INFORMATION ACCESS POINTS

Information access points (IAPs) fall between the cyber cafe and telecenter approaches. They have the narrow focus on the Internet and Web but tend to have a public service mandate. The most dramatic example is Canada's Community Access Program that established 10,000 access points in rural and urban areas across the country between 1994 and 2001. Computers and network connections were placed in community centers, libraries, schools, and other public places in order to make Canada the most interconnected country in the world.

Canada's success has energized other IAP initiatives. In 2002 the government of Mexico began establishing a network of Centros Comunitarios Digitales as part of its Sistema Nacional e-Mexico; simultaneously, across the world, in the state of Tamil Nadu, the Sustainable Access in Rural India (SARI) project involved an effort to set up kiosks in up to 100 villages in Madurai District as the first phase of an initiative that will see thousands of IAP kiosks flooding villages all over the state. Sectorally oriented agencies such as the World Health Organization have taken steps toward creating specialized portals and related IAPs.

FROM SERVICE TO ACCESS

Telephone service is a good place to start a review of the background of telecenters, because physical telephone lines initially were the principal local medium for connecting computerstothe worldwide Internet system. Telecommunications specialists use the term universal service to describe the individual household ownership pattern of telephone ownership. In spite of the ubiquity of the cell phone, it is apparent that, for a variety of reasons, most of the world's population will not experience anything close to universal service for at least another generation.

The more viable strategy for developing countries is universal access-an approach that says that a telephone should be within a reasonable distance for everyone. That distance would vary according to factors such as available transportation, road systems, and geography. "Reasonable distance" in Brazil is to be within five kilometers of a telephone; in South Africa, the standard is a thirty-minute traveling distance to the phone; and in China, it is "one family, one telephone in urban areas and telephone service to every administrative village in rural areas". Canada's International Development Research Center (IDRC., which is especially active in the field of information and communication technologies in Africa, uses "an hour's journey on foot" as the criterion for reasonable distance.

Proximity is not the only important factor. Regarding the telephone, there is also the cost and availability of the equipment and the availability of telephone lines. Developing countries have a much smaller density of telephone lines than industrialized nations. Typically the teledensity of African countries is one to two lines per 100 people. In Egypt it is eight, Europe forty-five, and the United States sixty-five. So, implicit in the concept of universal access is the idea of sharing a connection or facility. The most obvious example is the public telephone booth or telephone-calling center.

Originally the concept of universal access was applied specifically to telephone use. However, the process of providing access and sharing facilities has been used in other areas of telecommunications. For example, community television viewing has been institutionalized in some countries such as India where the government provides community television sets for the rural population. As computers and then the Internet led the shaping of the information society, the concept of universal access has been applied to these ICTs. The principal solution for providing universal access to information technologies has been the establishment of some kind of community-based telecenter, where the idea of sharing ICT facilities is a dominant feature.

E-DEVELOPMENT

ICTs have become an important component of national and community development, such that some countries such as India, Australia, and Malaysia have developed national ICT policies to get their populations and institutions connected. As we shall see below, international development agencies have taken a key role in developing nations because of the advantages they see associated with ICTs. Information technologies have played a role in development for at least half a century. Rural radio forums, a product of the 1950s, continue today in some countries.

Audio and videocassette technology, along with broadcasting, satellites, and various audio-visual technologies, became part of the development communication tool kit in the last half of the twentieth century. Heavily influencing the communication technology initiatives was an interest in distance learning projects. For example, very early in this history was Radio Sutatenza, which began educational and cultural programming in Colombia in 1947. One of the most dramatic events in the half-century was the use of a communication satellite in India to provide television programs to the six most underdeveloped areas of the country.

Although radio and television continue to be important "new technologies" for some parts of the world, computers and the Internet are attracting substantial interest in development for a variety of reasons. Much of this comes because of the dramatic technical advances in communication and computer hardware in the last decade, along with the interest of many governments in privatization and microenterprises.

Other factors include the vast amount of material potentially available on demand through the World Wide Web (www) and other networks-information ranging from local market prices to health information; and some ICTs offer interactivity so that people can address distant experts, officials, or relatives, rather than only being passive receivers.

And personal needs can be met through individual operation of some ICT instruments. Applying some of these ICT benefits especially to conditions across the developing world, Van Crowder (1998) notes that services offered by telecenters are a part of the solution to problems that rural communities and development agencies aim to solve. By providing access to accurate and timely information, "telecenters offer communities opportunities to:

- Reduce the isolation and marginalization of rural communities;
- Facilitate dialogue between rural communities and those who influence them, such as government planners, development agencies, researchers, technical experts, educators, etc.;
- Encourage participation of rural communities in decision making which impacts their lives;
- Coordinate development efforts in local regions for increased efficiency and effectiveness;
- Share experience, knowledge, and 'lessons learned' with other rural communities to address issues within local contexts;
- Provide information, training resources and programs when needed in a responsive, flexible manner [including, for example, resources related to agriculture, health, nutrition, and small business entrepreneurship];
- Facilitate ongoing development initiatives aimed at solving a variety of problems;
- Improve communication among stakeholders, thus overcoming the physical and financial barriers that often prevent researchers, extension workers, farmers and others from sharing knowledge and competence."

THE INTERNATIONAL INITIATIVES

The central and vital role communication and information play in the lives of people was officially recognized by the U.N. General Assembly in December 1997 when it endorsed a statement on the Universal Access to Basic Communication and Information Services. The statement concluded that the "introduction and use of information and communication technology must become a priority effort of the United Nations in order to secure sustainable human development." The statement also embraced the objective of establishing "universal access to basic communication and information services for all".

In mid-2000, the eight major industrial nations (the G-8) acknowledged that ICT "is one of the most potent forces in shaping the twenty-first century [and] its revolutionary impact affects the way people live, learn and work, and the way government interacts with civil society." Emerging from the discussion was the Okinawa Charter on the Global Information Society. Its framers announced that "this Charter represents a call to all, in both the public and private sectors, to bridge the international information and knowledge divide."

The Charter also renewed a commitment of the G-8 nations "to the principle of inclusion: everyone everywhere should be enabled to participate in and no one should be excluded from the benefits of the global information society". The G-8 launched a major effort to strengthen all nations' potential to be part of this Information Age starting with a Digital Opportunity Task Force (DOT) which reported to the G-8 in mid-2001. In its final report Digital Opportunities for All: Meeting the Challenge, the DOT noted the relationship between high priority international development goals and communication and emphasized that harnessing the power of information and communication technologies (ICT) could contribute substantially to realizing every one of these goals.

It could happen either directly (e.g., through greater availability of health and reproductive information, training of medical personnel and teachers, giving opportunity and voice to women, and expanding access to education and training) or indirectly (through creating new economic opportunities that lift individuals, communities, and nations out of poverty). The first stage of the effort to help people gain the benefits of new information and communication technology has been heavily devoted to institution building and connectivity, that is, the physical links between people and the digital world.

These efforts have ranged from making computers available and creating Internet service providers (ISP) to inventing innovative ways of establishing the telecommunications links. Telecenter development has been part of this effort. The Dot Force plan of action includes four principal directions for action. One deals with connectivity issues; the other three deal with nonhardware issues such as policy, capacity building, and developing appropriate content.

We should emphasize here that the initiatives directed toward ICT development are relevant to telecenters, cyber cafes, and IAPs because, for a majority of the world's population, for a long time, these local establishments may be many people's only entry into cyberspace and the benefits of ICT. In October 2001, the United Nations Development Program (UNDP) provided a "fast-track follow-up" to the G-8 action-plan by launching a Trust Fund for Information and Communication Technology for Development, with the Japanese government making the first contribution of US$5 million.

Two programs supported by the World Bank are important in the telecenter movement in providing a supportive cyber environment. These are recent initiatives of infoDev, a multidonor unit in the World Bank's Global Information and Communications department info Dev has a mandate to promote the use of ICT for social and economic development. The programs are "e-Readiness" and "Country Gateways," and they are especially relevant to building a supportive environment for telecenters.

E-READINESS

E-Readiness is an assessment of a country's status regarding ICT infrastructure, the accessibility of ICT to the population, the suitability of the policy environment for ICT effectiveness, and everyday use of ICT. The infoDev program has become a major provider of funding to countries that want to do such assessments. By the end of 2001 more than 130 assessments had been undertaken (with various funding), with repetition as many as six times in some countries. The key actors in doing or supporting e-Readiness studies in addition to infoDev are the UNDP, the World Economic Forum (WEF), the International Telecommunications Union, USAID, and the U.K. Department for International Development.

More than fifteen e-Readiness assessment tools have been many e-Readiness assessments but virtually no action. Another challenge in the e-Readiness world is gathering reliable data at the local level and building appropriate programs there. The Global Network Readiness Project, a joint project of Harvard's Center for International Studies, the Markle Foundation, the WEF, IBM, the UNDP, and the United Nations Foundation, is forming a network of experts to provide advice to nations interested in moving into concrete strategies.

In September 2001, infoDev announced a Country Gateways program and allocated US$1.8 million for its first fiscal year. It is a partner to the World Bank's Development Gateway initiative which is directed by the Development Gateway Foundation, a public-private partnership created in December 2001 and whose board of directors represents civil society and public and private donors.

The Development Gateway is an Internet portal for information on sustainable development and poverty reduction and expects to help fill the knowledge and communication needs of government officials and promote government quality and efficiency by providing information on best practices, networks for sharing solutions and experiences, and tools for analysis and problem solving. Its search engine is dedicated to helping public, civil society, and private sector people navigate the Internet to find useful information and resources.

For example, if officials in a community in a developing nation want to attract investors to the community, then they need to advertise the community's assets and provide legal information and data on infrastructure and the local labour market. The gateway provides an international platform for diffusing this information widely. When it was first introduced, the gateway stirred up substantial controversies because some perceived it as a "super-site" and a gatekeeper on development information, and some thought its management and control might not be impartial and beneficial to all. "A measure of success of the Development Gateway Foundation," says a World Bank official "will be how much it helps connect existing Internet portals and networks and brings together more resources for government, civil society, and donor agency ICT initiatives."

The Country Gateways are independently owned and operated partners of the Development Gateway. Each gateway is designed to provide country-level information and resources and promote local content development and knowledge sharing. In some cases, Country Gateways will provide e-government, e-business, and e-learning, and, overall, contribute to better connectivity and use of ICT. infoDev provides funding for planning of gateways (an average of US$50,000, but up to US$100,000) and may also provide funding for start-up activity.

MAJOR CHALLENGES FOR THE TELECENTER MOVEMENT

In general, the telecommunications professionals have made enormous advances in connectivity. Hudson (2002) suggests that several new technologies offer the potential for developing countries to bypass wireline networks and use facilities (such as satellites) to provide connectivity, even in remote and isolated areas that will be long out of the reach of terrestrial networks.

In the next stage of telecenter development, initiatives will need to concentrate on how to use ICTs and telecenters effectively for development. The question of telecenter effectiveness merges into a discussion of sustainability and viability-significant subjects that are woven throughout telecenter planning. This chapter offers a list of factors vital to telecenter sustainability that will need to be explored further.

One of the biggest challenges telecenters face is providing relevant information and services for their stakeholders. To survive, telecenters must be substantially demand driven whatever their sources of income. This translates into the need to have relevant and useful content. Some organizations-such as the Country Gateways are working on the content problems, but much of the information available via electronic networks may not meet communities' needs for local and localized information on agriculture, health, entrepreneurship and jobs, and nearby markets.

A telecenter may also have low relevance if information is in unfamiliar or inappropriate language or dialects. For example, while there are more than 12,000 Web page listings under "health" on the Internet, the material is useless to many because most of it is in English and much is expressed in ways unfamiliar even to English speakers in Kenyan towns and villages. A case in India shows how the staff of a "village knowledge center" dealt with the issues of relevance and language. The M.S. Swaminathan Research Foundation (MSSRF) was convinced that the local people had the capacity to absorb the new communication technology, but the question was: Can people get the information they need and want in the way they want it?

The centers established by MSSRF demonstrated ingenuity, creativity, and sensitivity in developing their information products. In one case, because some villagers were not literate, computer network information such as weather reports was downloaded as audio files. These audio files were then played on loudspeakers in front of the centers. In addition, project volunteers in the villages built their own databases to go with those external sources to provide local information on agricultural, health, and government programs for low-income people.

The clustering of telecenters in some fashion can help support a "value addition center." MSSRF has made this arrangement, and the cost of producing local information is spread over a number of telecenters. This issue is addressed in another context in the following section. A commitment by policy makers to telecenter development, and following that commitment with funding and organizational support for multiyear programs.

The Canadian government went beyond the rhetoric of an information society and committed people and funding to making the Internet affordable in rural and urban communities across the nation through community access points. It made a six-year commitment, providing startup money and an infrastructure to help local organizations make it work. While the resources offered are not enough for a complete comprehensive multipurpose telecenter, the imprimatur of the national government combined with a substantial amount of money significantly motivated a nationwide community-based effort that commanded provincial, regional, and local participation.

Similarly, in Australia the federal government's move to create the "Networking the Nation" fund has been instrumental in Tasmania's development of fifty-nine Open Access Centers and a program in New South Wales to set up fifty-five multipurpose "Technology Centers". In South Africa, the 1996 Telecommunications Act created the Universal Service Agency, which has been the key actor in establishing and funding telecenters in underserved and rural areas of the country.

Besides the direct funding available and the administrative push, a national policy can also be instrumental in providing a favorable regulatory and tariff climate and in producing the human resources that are vital to a telecenter movement. For example, to support its policy goal of becoming an information society superpower, the Indian government doubled the number of persons it would graduate from its technology training institutes. The Egyptian government's plan for incorporating ICTs in its business and socioeconomic development includes-besides Technology Access Community Centers in rural areas-creation of facilities in all its twenty-seven provinces that can train 30,000 people annually in computer uses.

Sustainability and government policy are often closely related. For example, governments are being urged to make policies that will enable communities to take greater advantage of ICTs. In December 2001, the state of Alaska persuaded the U.S. federal government to allow schools with low-cost subsidized Internet connections to use the same facility, with its excess capacity, for the community during after-school hours. This allows Alaskans in remote communities without toll-free dial-up service to have an affordable telecenter by "piggybacking" on the Internet access that is already available in schools that, as in many rural areas, are already the center of their communities.

National policy and national government funding do not necessarily translate into centralized planning and operations. Hungary has demonstrated that a former socialist country steeped in centralized planning could develop a "telecottage" system built on local nongovernmental organizations (NGOs) with community ownership and management. It is called a civic initiative with its emphasis on local NGOs applying for government telecottage grants and showing that they have the support of local governments or private organizations.

Where are the universities? One of the oddest characteristics of the telecenter movement is the absence of universities as partners in the production and packaging of research-based factual information, even though many universities have been very active on the technical side, including, for example, India's Institutes of Technology and the Massachusetts Institute of Technology's Media Lab.

The social role of the university historically has been to create, store, and diffuse knowledge, a collection of activities that partially parallels some telecenter operations. Yet, few major programs link telecenters to universities as an institutionalized source of information. Universities could play a significantly broader role in the world's efforts to employ ICTs for sustainable development and poverty reduction. For example, universities could

- Conduct continual research on community information needs so that appropriate information resources can be developed.
- Conduct on-going e-Readiness studies at the regional and community level and interpret their results for regional and local policy formulation and action.

- Convert their own research and academic knowledge into education, information, and training packages suitable for community use.
- Mobilize, interpret, integrate, and package information from external authoritative sources and tailor it to the needs of populations in surrounding communities.
- Train students in the application of ICTs to development problems by assigning them as student interns at community telecenters, having them collect indigenous case studies and "lessons learned" related to development initiatives, involving them in data collection and processing related to e-Readiness and information needs analysis studies, and training them in the process of information packaging.
- Design and execute ICT training programs for various community groups, especially those that are likely to be bypassed by conventional ICT training.
- Through their participation as students in this program, prepare a new generation of professionals in various sectors to use and support the application of ICTs and telecenters for community development and poverty alleviation programs.
- Provide ongoing monitoring and evaluation support to ICT initiatives.
- Actively contribute to the Country Gateway system.
- Orient university officials and faculty to ICT-for-development so they can be opinion leaders in this area.

A small start is being made in India where the University of Veterinary and Animal Sciences (TANUVAS) is revamping some of its extension centers to make them support units for village information centers. While telecenter patrons in the villages can access Web pages from far distant places, they will also have available information from the university's research labs, packaged to their needs by the TANUVAS information support unit.

Some universities already have experience and commitments that are relevant to community development information and training through ICTs and telecenters. For example, universities have been involved in extension, a system designed to link researchers with potential users of their research. And since the days of correspondence courses, universities have used a variety of media for distance learning, especially focusing on formal education at secondary school and college levels.

However, few universities have yet taken the step toward linking their knowledge resources to telecenters and to the potential of ICT for development. Headway was made in mid-2001 when several universities became involved in the new Country Gateway activities. For example, universities in West Bank and Gaza, the Dominican Republic, Rwanda, and Nicaragua received planning grants from the infoDev program to host country gateways.

The main reason for the extraordinary reputation of the Gasaleka Telecenter as one of the most active and vibrant in South Africa is Masilo Mokobane, director of the project. In spite of nagging infrastructure and economic problems, he is a telecenter visionary. From the first day, Mokobane has not only been fighting for survival of the center, but he has also been entertaining new ideas to better serve his community through the use of new communication technologies. He personifies what we call a champion.

The obscurity and abstractness of the information society requires the missionary zeal of individuals who can translate and demonstrate the relevance and application of these kinds of concepts to the realities of the community. For the innovator to be from the community itself increases the credibility and potential diffusion of the telecenter initiative.

In most communities, volunteers offer a variety of benefits to multipurpose telecenters. They contribute to the day-in, day-out supervision of the facilities a potential personnel expense that many could not otherwise afford. The volunteer, however, has deeper significance: the variety of volunteers in a system provides telecenter clientele with personal models with whom they can identify and feel comfortable. In telecenters throughout the world, one can find high school and college students, retired business people, active and retired school teachers, and others providing one-on-one and group training and assistance. Volunteers can also contribute to enlightened decision making in the telecenter because they reflect a variety of community constituencies.

The challenge for telecenters is to move from largely spontaneous use and management of volunteers to developing an explicit strategic plan for recruiting, training, retaining, and rewarding volunteers. Trish Barren in Western Australia's Telecenter Support Unit summarizes the volunteer issue in three words: "Gain, Train, and Retain." The important issue is to find incentives to fit the kind of volunteers available. For some it is the recognition, for others it is free time on the computers, and for others it may be college credits in the local university.

The Western Australia Telecenter Network Support Unit illustrates well what can be done when telecenters are combined in some way so that they share a support system. The support unit lobbies, seeks funding, develops initiatives, and carries out a variety of other management functions for the seventy-six members of the network. As Kyle (2001) and Gáspár (2001) point out from their experiences in Hungary and Brazil, opportunities for expanding content-related services such as tele-agriculture, tele-business, and tele-culture are more affordable when serving multiple units.

Architects of telecenter systems can build such support components into their systems and devise a method for funding them, such as membership fees. One of the major recommendations to the government of India (GOI) that came out of a 2001 national ICT workshop in Chennai was that the GOI foster the establishment of an NGO National Association of Telecenters, similar to those being developed in Hungary and Australia. The recommendation included the following list of tasks for such an association:

- Coordinate content supply with developers and suppliers.
- Negotiate with resource suppliers such as companies selling computers and related equipment.
- Arrange public relations advocacy and awareness campaigns

for ICT and telecenters.

- Provide liaison with government departments and NGOs.
- Train telecenter personnel and organizational users of telecenter facilities.
- Promote and support practical research and evaluation for telecenter operations.
- Provide liaison and negotiating with other communication enterprises (for example, cable television operators, radio broadcasting organizations).
- Provide leadership and enforcement of minimum standards of service and professional codes of conduct.

An addition to this list could be: collecting, archiving, and diffusing information on telecenters (possibly in collaboration with a country gateway). Stories abound about the difference that access to information technologies makes in the lives of individuals and communities. A woman in India who complained about her vision (she said it was like having a saree over her eye) learned at a telecenter about a traveling health team visiting her area.

She had a simple operation and the "saree" (cataract) was removed. Another story is about the farmer in northern Shaanxi Province in China who traveled 500 kilometers to an agricultural information center where he found information online that helped him profitably market his apples and start up a pumpkin export trade. Despite the anecdotal success stories about ICTs and telecenters, there is still widespread lack of understanding about the role and benefits of information technologies. And skeptics were reinforced by computer giant Bill Gates, who startled many in the information technology field when he declared in the Guardian newspaper, "the world's poorest two billion people desperately need health care, not laptops".

Malaysia's National Information Technology Council recognizes the challenge in establishing a community's awareness of the benefits of information. Its vision is "to evolve a value-based knowledge society in the Malaysian mould where the society is rich in information, empowered by knowledge, infused with a distinctive value-system, and is self-governing." So, high on its strategic agenda is an effort to develop a national mindset that includes making Malaysians aware of the emerging e-world and enabling the diffusion and acculturation of ICT at the grassroots level.

Government or private-sector initiatives targeting popular participation in the information society will need to consider carrying out vigorous campaigns to illustrate the benefits of information as an important resource for daily living-assuming they themselves are reasonably convinced. As the Malaysians suggest, the target includes producing "ICT-fluent" professionals, including leaders in education and government. The importance of awareness rising was illustrated in Korea.

In November 2001 a conference was held there related to gender and ICTs. Given the recent release of a major study indicating the importance of ICTs and telecenters for women in developing nations, the authors asked a participant to report to them on the outlook of women attending the program. She comments:

The thing that was wonderful was that the women suddenly realised that the Telecenter Movement was so powerful, not just another project but a movement that they could collectively use to make their voices heard while assisting their communities. They realized that this was a tool which was readily available to change things and make a difference and that they could be a part of it.

Information and public relations campaigns promoting telecenters are part of the solution, but the parallel challenge lies in the appropriate development of services. Telecenters can systematically assess community information needs and the communication needs of various local organizations and be creative and entrepreneurial in dealing with these needs. This more comprehensive community service approach to the information society helps centers become more firmly woven into the fabric of the community and puts them on the road to self-sufficiency.

RESEARCH AS A TELECENTER MANAGEMENT TOOL

Research for needs assessment and project evaluation is an important component of telecenter operations, because a research program provides the tools to meet community needs and monitor the financial viability of the telecenter. Research is not a common practice in telecenter deployment, however. Even though many telecenter endeavors are self-labeled as research and development or pilot projects, not many of these projects carry a rigorous research program. Research for needs assessment and evaluation should be integrated as a natural component of any telecenter project, not just internationally funded initiatives with a mandate to produce feasibility studies and evaluation reports.

Telecenter personnel should have simple, reliable tools to use in ongoing operations-tools that (1) help them discover and continuously monitor the needs of the community, (2) get a reliable picture of the demographics of the area, (3) systematically monitor ongoing operations, and (4) check on outcomes and consequences. This goes beyond counting the number of users, although the number of users is an important statistic.

Resolving tensions in the field is sometimes as important as any methodological concerns about measurement or sampling. For example, there may be significant conflicts between what the development practitioners think are the problems and the communication needs and what the community perceives, prioritizes, and demands.

Other than urban cyber cafes, most telecenters operate in a not-for-profit mode, but that does not mean not-for-income. Typically donor agencies reduce or discontinue financial support for telecenters after an initial incubation period. Gumucio-Dagron (2001) argues that telecenters that have a mandate to contribute to a community's welfare should not be responsible for their own full financial support any more than a community library is. Proenza (2001) offers a contrasting view in suggesting that telecenters should be more rigorous about adopting business models. Perhaps the answer is the compromise that telecenters need to have a financial plan for whatever the sources of support will be.

Telecenter systems have been innovative in developing income-producing activities to support telecenter operations. Among the telecottages in Hungary, there are more than fifty different services offered to the community. A major source of support for telecottages is the contracts that they obtain from government agencies, thus becoming (for a fee) extensions for government services. The Queensland (Australia. Open Learning Network's Learning Centres offer training courses that are paid for by trainees' employers or by the individuals themselves. Businesses and industry groups pay for use of the teleconferencing facilities, and institutions in the community pay membership fees to the centers.

In this research on telecenter training (in which the authors surveyed a panel of experts from around the world), one of the most frequently suggested areas of training for telecenter managers was in the area of business planning aimed at making telecenters self-sufficient and sustainable. In approaching the issue of sustainability, telecenters face the question of how they can generate income yet serve those in the community who cannot afford to pay for "public goods" kinds of services (such as access to health information). Some centers use the income from user fees and other income services to make public goods more affordable or free.

GAINING COMMUNITY PARTICIPATION

With widespread interest in the "digital divide" issue, broad-based community participation may become part of a telecenter's mandate. This may present a challenge in reaching out to ethnic minorities, women, children, and the elderly, who are often on the minus side of the divide. Sometimes the learning label on a center, the technology, or its location in a library or school intimidates those who might benefit from the services. Physical connectivity, then, may not equal sociological access.

It is generally accepted that conscientious attention to participation can yield benefits in such activities as assessment of information needs, planning, and operations. The value of participation is woven throughout the Hungarian and Brazilian experience with telecenters. Yet, one of the most underappreciated aspects of the participation issue is that it is not a spontaneous phenomenon. Part of the problem results from the ambiguity of the participation concept and the need to translate it into concrete action terms. Briefly, the strategy should be explicit and address at least the following questions:

- Why is participation important to this project?
- Who should participate?
- How might people participate?
- How much participation should be sought?
- When should participation take place?
- What incentives can be offered?

At the beginning of this chapter we mentioned the three major tracks for bringing ICTs to communities in a universal access approach to connectivity. There is considerable chance that the future of these enterprises will intersect as each tries to find a stable place in this rapidly changing digital world. As IAPs multiply by the thousands, we can predict that community demand-ignited by the discovery that information and communication have value will persuade many of them to expand their services and change into multipurpose telecenters.

Telecenters might also look at the culture of the cyber cafe to see what other features could be adopted profitably by the telecenter. For example, in many places the ambiance of the cyber cafe is social and pleasurable: the cafe aspect is an important attraction for the persons who frequent the places.

Computer games are popular. Even in fulfilling their development communication objectives, telecenters will need to recognize the importance of being a nice place to visit. Despite its commercial and narrow interests, the cyber cafe phenomenon is important in the context of telecenters, because cyber cafes may discover that some development-related services are, in fact, profitable.

3

Methodologies for Systems Design and Evaluation

ICTs threaten to expand the already wide socioeconomic gap between urban and rural populations in developing countries while simultaneously offering opportunities to reduce it. This chapter describes research into the implementation and operation of rural telecenters in two locations in India and Malaysia, funded by Canada's International Development Research Center (IDRC).

The research demonstrates how methodologies for ICT implementation can be successfully adapted to the development challenges faced by rural communities and how such implementations can be evaluated so that the often unexpected and desirable results that emerge can be revealed and accounted for. The results described in this chapter suggest novel approaches to system implementation methodologies for rural development and outcome evaluation that challenge traditional wisdom in the implementation of information systems.

ICTS AND DEVELOPMENT

There is growing enthusiasm in the development community over the potential for contemporary Information and Communication Technologies (ICTs) to alleviate some of the social and economic problems of the developing world. A decade ago, the World Bank was reporting that Information

Technology (IT) "is the driving force for a new techno-economic paradigm with far reaching effects for all types of industries and services and for the competitive position of developing countries." Apparently, "developing countries at all levels of development must stay abreast of the information revolution".

IT is important for developing countries in alleviating information poverty, enhancing competitiveness, improving public sector management, participating in global trade and production, and promoting environmentally friendly development. Developing countries must see the development and effective use of their information infrastructure as a key national objective. According to Nelson Mandela, "eliminating the distinction between information rich and information poor countries is critical to eliminating other inequalities between North and South and to improving the quality of life of all humanity".

Despite the acknowledged potential for ICT-induced development, access to the technologies remains heavily skewed in favour of the world's developed nations. The United Nations reports that the technology gap and related inequities between industrialized and developing nations are widening and a new type of poverty, information poverty, looms. This is further complicated by the emergence of new information elitism both among and within countries.

Developing countries are threatened by domination, marginalization, and even exclusion. In 1993, high-income economies with 15 per cent of the world's population had 71 per cent of the world's telephone lines, and this disparity has hardly changed in the last decade. More than 90 per cent of IT production takes place in Organization for Economic Cooperation and Development (OECD) countries and the average high-income economy has more than 100 times more computers per capita than the average low-income economy.

Closer scrutiny of the disparities in the global distribution of ICTs reveals that the least served sections of society are the rural areas of developing countries, where the majority of the world's population live. In most developing countries, the vast majority of the population still live in rural areas 71 per cent of their total population, according to the World Bank. There is a gap in access to telecommunications facilities between urban and rural areas, and IT has been used almost exclusively to benefit urban areas. In some least developed countries, the rural telephone main line density is lower than 1 per 1000, with large areas of territory not having any telephones.

Development agencies acknowledge the imperative of rural access to ICTs in achieving sustainable development. The United Nations Development Program (UNDP) suggests that strengthening rural telecommunications must be treated as a central parameter for any sustainable human development strategy aimed at poverty alleviation and reduction. The World Bank emphasizes the need to expand access to information for poor villages and to allow them to participate in markets and to monitor local government.

McNamara points out that access to information is essential for the development of rural areas and rural communities are often prepared to spend a larger portion of their income on communications. Benefits per telephone are likely to be greater where density is lowest. The greatest payoff from telecommunications investment, therefore, may be in rural and isolated areas. The International Telecommunication Union has pointed out that rural and remote areas of most developing countries have less population density and suffer from an almost complete lack of telecommunication infrastructures.

Telecommunication and information technologies, it says, are a means to accelerate the growth of the rural economy that subsequently helps in alleviating poverty and in improving living conditions in rural areas. In devising strategies for providing rural communities, especially those in developing countries, with access to ICTs, the UNDP notes that one of the most promising approaches might be the provision of rural telecommunications services on a community basis organized in the form of a public utility. Such utilities are often termed telecenters.

One definition of telecenters is a physical space that provides public access to ICTs for educational, personal, social, and economic development. Telecenters are designed to provide a combination of ICT services, ranging from basic telephone or e-mail service to full Internet/World Wide Web connectivity. Demand for telecommunications services, even among people with very low annual incomes, is evidenced by the phenomenal growth of small telecenters, which are now mushrooming in many countries.

Telecenters are springing up in Africa, Latin America, and Asia. Telecenters take the form of public-access facilities to provide electronic communications services, especially in marginalized or remote areas where commercial development of ICTs is not prevalent. Alongside the spread of telecenters, practitioners and researchers are questioning how best they can be used to alleviate the problems of rural life in developing countries. Despite much anecdotal evidence, there is yet very little experience of the impact of such centers in the context of rural and remote areas in developing countries, and many questions need to be answered before embarking on ambitious and costly programs at a national level.

Among the questions, Ernberg asks how it is possible to help people participate effectively in the production of information and knowledge relevant to them and how to assess the social impact of different applications such as telemedicine and government and community information systems. Such questions, among others, are beginning to be taken up by a loose grouping of development workers and academics that practice what has become known as community informatics. Community informatics pays attention to physical communities and the design and implementation of technologies and applications, which enhance and promote their objectives.

Studies in community informatics show how ICTs can help achieve a community's social, economic, political, or cultural goals. Community informatics is especially relevant to the deployment of ICTs to rural communities in developing countries where numbers of telecenters are being installed and where the predominant model of one person per computer that exists in the developed world is least likely to prevail. Gurstein points out that community informatics is concerned with how to design electronically enabled services, and he suggests a model for an integrated service delivery system that includes:

- A community-based technical capacity to receive services and information.
- A social/organizational capacity to receive and redistribute services and information.
- An organizational capacity to localize external information.
- A technical capacity to mount and deliver this information.
- A human capacity to mobilize resources, including leadership and vision.
- A social and organizational capacity to utilize and implement the services and information provided
- An overall program development and management capability.
- A measure to ensure evaluation and feedback from the service and information.

Accordingly, community informatics can be seen as a set of integrated disciplines that embed ICTs fully within the functioning of a community. It accounts for the design of the social system in which the technology is embedded as well as the technology system with which it interacts. Community informatics thus is an extension from organizations to communities of the sociotechnical approach to systems design.

This favors a social systems approach, whereby the emphasis is placed on the context within which the system will be embedded, the interactions between that context and the system and how each influences the other. This approach recognizes that the act of trying to solve a problem, especially an organizational problem, actually changes the nature of the problem, as organizations are essentially social systems with their own cultural and social dynamics.

The design and implementation of information systems has long been practiced as a discipline by systems analysts utilizing one of many available methodologies as a guide for eliciting the information processing requirements of the users of a system and for expressing them in a manner that facilitates the construction of the requisite system. Historically, the design of methodologies for the development of information systems has been directed at improving the processes of management, usually expressed in terms of organizational efficiency, effectiveness, competitiveness, or some other form of relative advantage.

Community informatics changes the context of systems development from the organization to the community, implying a perspective of information systems development with the following elements:

- That information systems are more than technical artifacts, as they embrace the behaviours and aspirations of the people using them.
- That information systems are spreading beyond formal organizations and into society at large.
- That our interpretations of information systems, and the formulas that are applied to designing them, assume a structured context that is not in fact always present.
- A focus on the uses to which IT is actually put that is independent of the intentions or aspirations of the providers of the technology, rather than on the institutional interests that often accompany the deployment of such technology.
- An interest in communities of users and the influence on the technology of the social dynamics of such communities, in conjunction with a recognition of the diversity of interests within such communities.
- A conviction that ICTs have the potential to empower or liberate individuals, groups, and communities, but that attention has so far been directed primarily to the goals of increased efficiency, control, and effectiveness.
- A desire to promote creative and enabling applications of information and communication technologies that extend the scope of information systems in ways that empower and enfranchise presently excluded or marginalized individuals or groups.
- A preference for collaborative and participative modes of inquiry and system development.

These elements of information systems development carry implications for the design and operation of methodological approaches that have yet to be fully articulated in formal specifications of particular system development methodologies. Methodologies have value in that they render systems design as less of an art and more of a structured process that imbues a high level of confidence in the efficacy of the design of a system prior to its construction and implementation.

Clearly systems development processes for community informatics will benefit if they too can assure development practitioners and community members that information systems will deliver their development potential to the full. The sociotechnical approach to information systems offers some of these assurances, acknowledging as it does that the context of systems implementations will inevitably shape and be shaped by the system and the processes adopted for its design. In addition, when blended with recent practices in development, such as Participatory Rural Appraisal and its cousins, methodological pointers begin to emerge that seem to be capable of guiding the application of community informatics toward successful implementations of rural ICTs in developing countries.

The following sections describe two components of a community informatics approach to systems development for rural communities in two developing countries, Malaysia and India. The first component relates to systems design and is taken from the Malaysian example, whereas the second component relates to systems evaluation and is taken from the Indian example.

UNDERSTANDING THE INFORMATION NEEDS

The first component of a community informatics approach to systems development for rural communities in developing countries comes from a research project entitled "Internet Access for Remote Communities in Sarawak, " funded by the Canadian IDRC. Sarawak is one of two Malaysian states on the island of Borneo. It is characterized by its diffused population spread across hilly and forested terrain with an underdeveloped infrastructure. The research took place against the background of Malaysia's enthusiasm for ICT-induced development initiatives.

The objective was to understand how ICTs could be used directly to achieve sustainable human development in rural areas. The site of the project is in a remote and isolated community of Bario where any form of ICT is nonexistent. The project's long-term goal is to stimulate rural development within the community by facilitating communication and access to information and learning resources as well as to stimulate local capacity for informed decision making and to enhance personal, institutional, and community development in the areas of agriculture, health, education, commerce, and governance. One expected outcome of the research project is the creation of a network of information systems that will facilitate sustainable development for the community.

The "nerve center" of this information system is a telecenter, which will serve as a community resource for the members of the community to use computers, connect to the Internet, and use a variety of associated services that will affect sustainable social development of the community. The settlement of Bario is inaccessible by road and is normally reached by small twenty-seat aircraft operated by the Malaysian Airline System from the coastal town of Miri.

The community is predominantly made up of people of the Kelabit ethnic group, one of Sarawak's smallest among its twenty-six or so identifiable ethnic minorities. Forested mountains surround the plain in which the people cultivate wet rice. People in the older part of the settlement live in a traditional longhouse, containing two communal areas that run the length of the building. One contains a kitchen space for each household, whereas the other is used for formal occasions involving the whole community. In between, each household has its own private living apartments. Longhouses are the traditional form of dwelling on the island of Borneo.

In preparation for the establishment of the Bario telecenter, the project team conducted a baseline survey to establish the preexisting socioeconomic profile of the community. Data were gathered from 140 households in the Bario district during a survey that was conducted during September and October 1999. Among other information obtained, the survey gathered data on the patterns of information use in the community. The following data were obtained:

- The type and amount of information they would like to receive.
- The type and amount of information they are receiving now.
- The type and amount of information they are sending now.
- The sources and amount of information they receive from them now.
- The channels and amount of information they received from them now.

The survey data indicated that the community placed most importance on information relating to agricultural, medical, and religious practices. Information technology, job opportunities, government policies, and family matters rated slightly less important. Current patterns of information actually received were dominated by religious information, with agricultural and family matters ranking next.

Most information that is sent outside the community concerned families, with religious information ranking closely behind. Relatives were the major source of information, outranking others in terms of the amount of information received by the community, with community leaders next. In this respect, face-to-face contacts outweigh all others as channels of incoming information, with the radio, church congregation, and community meetings ranking about equally next.

Initially, a computer laboratory of ten personal computers (PCs) was set up in the junior secondary school and a teaching program for IT literacy installed. This was extended to interested community members after school hours. Subsequently, a temporary telecenter was established in the local lodge, which is a common meeting house for the community, pending the construction of a custom-designed building to house the telecenter. The telecenter was equipped with four PCs and two printers. Bario is off grid for electricity supply, and in both the school and the telecenter, additional electricity generators were provided to augment existing supplies.

All equipment had to be flown in by chartered aircraft. The telecenter was initially used to prepare documents for local events and administration. A manager was assigned reporting to the local project steering committee. Telekom Malaysia has partnered with the research project and has installed VSAT (Very Small Aperture Terminal) satellite equipment to connect the computers in the telecenter to the Internet. The researchers organized a symposium for community members and other Kelabit in order to identify and prioritize suitable information systems for use the Bario people.The researchers adopted the following guiding principles to design and implement information systems:

- Useful information systems will be embedded in the needs of the community.
- Specific actions are required by both the researchers and the community in order to articulate those needs.
- Participatory action research (PAR) encompasses a suitable set of principles for the conduct of the research.
- Methodologies for designing and implementing useful information systems will emerge from participatory action-oriented research activities.

In accordance with these principles, the Sarawak researchers adopted PAR as the main form of study. According to Mikkleson, action-oriented studies ask questions about how people act in accordance with knowledge that is accumulated and disseminated during the course of the research process. The criteria by which the quality of the research is judged are based on the extent to which change takes place and in what direction it occurs among the research subjects.

The researcher-researched relationship is characterized by a shifting between closeness and distance and the organization of the research is largely democratic and flexible. The research results are integrated into the study methods, and the perceptions of interest for the researchers are predominantly emancipating. Robert Chambers (1997) describes the term participatory action-reflection research as encompassing methods that combine action, reflection, participation, and research. PAR seeks to actively involve people in generating knowledge about their own condition and how it can be changed.

The techniques used in PAR include collective research through meetings, critical recovery of history, valuing and applying folk culture, and the production and diffusion of new knowledge through written, oral, and visual forms. Chambers claims that PAR has contributed five normative ideas to development research:

- Professionals should reflect critically on their concepts, values, behaviours, and methods.
- They should learn through engagement and committed action.
- They have roles as conveners, catalysts, and facilitators.
- The weak and marginalized can and should be empowered.
- Poor people can and should do much of their own investigation, analysis, and planning.

Gardner and Lewis characterize PAR as a loose group of methodologies whose main objective for development is the fulfillment of the human urge for engagement, rather than targeting poverty alleviation, basic needs, or structural change. In this way, PAR seeks to avoid the dependency that results from many external interventions. Typically, educated outsiders who encourage groups of people to get together and engage in their own social investigation bring about catalytic initiatives.

Eventually, as groups form links with other similar groups and encourage new ones, dependence on the internal-external stimulus falls away, though contact may be maintained. PAR provides constructive opportunities for the subjects of the research to tie the research agenda to their needs. Action research becomes a process in which research is combined with practical problem solving, with the participation of those who have identified and need to overcome a problem.

These descriptions of PAR resonate with the sociotechnical perspective of information systems that community informatics advocates. PAR is considered highly appropriate for development research that seeks to demonstrate the value of information and ICTs to communities in developing countries. Da vies underlines this observation by suggesting that the "revolution in information technology and communications has direct implications for the South and for development studies in the emergence of participatory methods for data collection and analysis.

Participatory techniques, just like changes in more conventional sources of information, are in part a result of-and dependent on-the international communications revolution." Within the PAR framework, the researchers in Sarawak have engaged community members to conduct surveys, perform interviews, adopt formal roles in the management of the research, participate in focus group meetings, and hold community gatherings to perform decision making and to direct the conduct of the research.

The symposium in Miri engaged members of the Bario community alongside relatives and other members of the Kelabit community in a participatory process combining problem definition, scenario painting, and information needs elicitation. The participating groups were facilitated by the researchers to agree on a prioritized set of information needs that make a significant impact on the development of Bario for the coming years. Arising from the experience, a number of key community members volunteered to progress the implementation of some of the development projects and to marshal the community resources necessary to achieve desirable outcomes.

For example, one of the Kelabit members living in Miri is a doctor and has agreed to provide teleconsulting services to the clinic in Bario. Another agreed to assemble and document best practices for production and treatment of Bario rice, a particular type of rice for which demand consistently outstrips supply throughout Sarawak.

Adopting PAR principles has led the researchers and the community in Malaysia to jointly agree on an agenda of systems development and implementation which would be associated with appropriate research to evaluate its effectiveness. In the Malaysian example, PAR seems to have facilitated the specification of a program of system implementation that is acceptable to the recipient community. In order to understand how best to evaluate the implementation of community systems, we turn to the experiences of another IDRC-supported project in India.

The information in this section comes from two telecenter projects in India, implemented by two organizations, the M.S. Swaminathan Research Foundation "Village Information Centers" in Pondicherry, and the Foundation of Occupational Development in Chennai. The IDRC organized a learning and evaluation study of the projects in November 1999. The evaluation took the form of a collection of stories told by the beneficiaries and users of the telecenters that had been implemented by each organization.The first project was developed by the M.S. Swaminathan Research Foundation as part of its program of taking the benefits of emerging and frontier technologies to the rural poor.

The researchers took the view that to be useful to farm families, the generic information found in networks, including the Internet, should be rendered into locality-specific knowledge that rural women and men can act on. This was the model adopted for implementation in this project. The foundation's approach to dissemination of new technologies in rural areas is premised on the statement of its founder, Professor M.S. Swaminathan: "Whatever a poor family can gain benefit from, the rich can also gain benefit; the reverse does not happen."

Thus, involvement of ultrapoor in rural areas (there are over 300 million ultrapoor in South Asia in managing the use of ICTs was considered essential for the success of this project. The other critical issue was the need to involve rural women.The project was started in 1998 in Pondicherry in South India because it has certain initial advantages: an accessible government and reasonable telecom infrastructure (urban teledensity of 20 app.). The level of poverty is high in rural areas, where about 21 per cent of the resident families have less than one U.S. dollar per day as family income. The objectives of this project were:

- Setting up village information shops that enable rural families access to a basket of modern information and communication technologies.
- Training educated youth, especially women, in rural areas in operating information shops.
- Training the rural youth in the organization and maintenance of a system that generates locally relevant information from generic information.
- Maintenance, updating, and dissemination of information on entitlements to rural families using an appropriate blend of modern and existing channels of communication.
- Conducting impact assessment based on organization of surveys, participatory rural appraisal, and other appropriate methods of data gathering.
- Building a model in information dissemination and exchange in rural areas that uses advanced information and communication technologies.

A value addition center was set up as an information hub in the village of Villianur, located in the western part of Pondicherry. A wireless hub was placed here and dial-up accounts to the Internet were also established. This was made the project office as well as an interface for the public and the government offices in the locality. Additional village centers were then set up in places where the community offered secure space, free of cost. A total of five such village centers were set up during the project period.

One of these is a village on the coast with 98 per cent of the population involved in fishing. The total population of the five villages is approximately 13,400 with about 47 per cent illiteracy. In each village center, a group of individuals identified by the community took charge of daily operations. They functioned as volunteers without receiving regular payments from the project. The village center operators were trained in PC operations and in using the data/voice network. They were trained in maintaining a register to log use of the center by the local residents. Training was also provided in the basics of management and in handling queries from illiterate individuals.

Regular contact was maintained between the operators and tne project staff. The project staff have designed and developed many locally useful databases:

- Entitlements to Rural Families: This database provides details of about 130 schemes that are operational in Pondicherry.
- Families Below the Poverty Line: The details of families in the communes of Ariyankuppam, Villianur, and Nettapakkam have been provided in this database that has been compiled from the administration and updated until April 2000. Approximately 22,000 families are listed. Being listed draws a number of entitlements.
- Grain prices in Pondicherry region (daily).
- Input prices (quality seeds and fertilizers) in Pondicherry region (daily).
- Directory of general and crop insurance schemes.
- Integrated Pest Management in rice crops.
- Pest management in sugarcane crop.
- Directory of hospitals and medical practitioners in Pondicherry grouped with specializations such as orthopedics and pediatrics.
- Bus and train timetables covering the Pondicherry region and two nearby towns.

Many of these databases are frequently updated, and some are updated even twice daily. Much of the information is accessed from local sources, on the Web, or otherwise. A critical portion comes from the Web, from national and international sources. All of them are transformed into locally useful material, in various formats (voice/digital audio, in some cases) and in the local language.

Tamil is spoken by 98 per cent of the population. The project staffs compiles useful information into daily bulletins and issues them on the network by e-mail.The centers receive an average of twelve visitors per day. The asset-less, ultrapoor families are among the major users. About 18 per cent of the users are women. These two results indicate the success of the project approach emphasizing the participation of women and the asset-less family.

The pattern of usage indicates those educational purposes (such as use of CD-ROMs) and accessing government data are the two most important uses of this system. In many instances local residents have derived benefits from the use of data and information derived from this network. Some of them are:

- Availing farm labour insurance by land-less women; 157 women obtained this insurance.
- School examination results and mark sheets downloaded from the Web; over the last two years about 2,100 students in all the centers have used this option and saved waiting time by at least one week per person.
- Ease of contacting medical practitioners and veterinarians: The local databases have been found specific and useful.
- Price information related to grain sales: This is the most important benefit according every farmer because it helps him or her to have a better negotiating position in dealing with price-fixing middlemen.
- Veerampattinam, a fishing hamlet, receives information on wave heights downloaded twice daily from the U.S. Naval Oceanographic laboratory. The craft-vessel fishermen view this as life saving.
- The largest number of users finds government sector data most useful; at least 147 individuals reported deriving benefits from housing schemes.

The variety and type of uses and subsequent benefits of use do not lend themselves to easy classification or methods of quantification in such a way that their impact can be understood and assessed. Consequently, the IDRC learning and evaluation study adopted an approach based on the collection of stories concerning the uses of the centers by the villagers. Stories, while anecdotal, offer a rich picture of the impact of ICT interventions in local, complex, and dynamic social settings. They are accessible and verifiable during short visits and they acknowledge the often indirect influence that development interventions have on the behaviour of their beneficiaries.

Moreover, stories as evaluation concede that the benefits of telecenter activities are often detectable only after they have been installed, contrary to traditional approaches to information systems, in which expected benefits are usually specified before the technology is installed. During visits to five village telecenters, the mission identified twenty-four separate success stories. Each story is specific to and reflective of the needs at a particular time of the community in which it was discovered. Each owes its outcome to the sensitive and timely delivery of useful information that contributed to local knowledge that facilitated something desirable for the recipient.

The success stories indicate in the depth and breadth of impact that ICTs have had within the target communities, that telecenters have the potential for contributing significantly to rural development. Within a PAR framework of implementation-evaluation-reflection-implementation, stories as evaluation serve two purposes. First they contribute to the action research cycle, by

- Guiding action, for example, by elaborating on baseline studies to reveal typical preexisting conditions within a community.
- Contributing to evaluation and continuous assessment by describing the evolving circumstances of the participants (researchers and community members) over time.
- Facilitating reflection by highlighting examples of outcomes and fostering a synthesis of their causes.

Second stories reveal the depth and breadth of the social context of the technology implementation, how social forces operate and intertwine, where the balance of influence and emphasis exists at certain crucial moments, how their relative influences contribute to desirable outcomes, and what the underlying trend is in their effectiveness. Some of the social forces that the authors believe define outcomes are:

COMMUNITY ASPIRATIONS

Experience suggests that technology cannot function successfully in the absence of some form of community ambition for a better life. Moreover, aspirations often need to be ignited, sometimes by an outside influence, and they need to be kindled and rekindled over time. The source of inspiration that sets off aspirations often changes during the introduction of technology, sometimes to unexpected sources, for example, school children, and there are usually many different sources at any one time.

LEARNING

The communities observed are all capable of learning new things, skills, ideas, and roles. They blend new information with preexisting knowledge and build it into something of lasting, perhaps growing, value to themselves. Learning seems to take place at all levels of the community, and its impact is accelerated by the rapid spread of new and useful knowledge within the community.

The pace of learning seems to accelerate as technology unfolds its capability and potential, further feeding the desire for new knowledge. People discover new facts themselves and they teach them to each other. The learning that occurs is usually deeper and more focused on real needs than the learning that is introduced from outside.

CAPACITIES

Learning often leads to expanded capacity, but this is of little value without the aspiration to take advantage of the extra capacity. The authors have observed in collecting the stories the pride that individuals take in the new roles and accomplishments that they have been able to achieve as a result of having their capacities expanded and their aspirations realized. The authors have also noticed that the processes that are specifically designed to achieve the results do not always trigger capacity building, for example, training. People seem to act as a result of a combination of circumstances, and if the right combination does not exist, any single factor in isolation may not be effective.

The extent to which a community is and remains organized seems to influence the use it can make of a telecenter. Community organization in this context relates to the role of coordinating the dynamics of the many social processes that occur simultaneously toward a desirable result. Telecenter activities impact all sections of a community, and they participate in many of the social processes that define its identity. Organization then is a function of harnessing the social dynamics of a community toward its own betterment, alongside, in our case, the introduction of new information. This usually requires some locus of community influence, but when new technologies are introduced this is often not the one occupied by the traditional leadership.

Many of the stories depict a sense of unity of purpose within the community that transcends the many differences that usually exist in any body of people. Desirable results emerge from, and contribute to, the unity of those affected, engendering a camaraderie that further acts on aspirations, capacity building, and organization.

Participation refers not only to the researcher-community relationships but also to the inclusion of all sections of the community. Stories that tell the most desirable outcomes indicate a will to include rather than to exclude sections of the community. Relative advantage is a less appealing benefit than is the greater good. Pride and its spinoffs (aspirations and capacity expansion) are nearly always evident when outcomes have a wide, inclusive impact. Individuals who achieve community-wide solutions earn respect and status. Those who exploit technology for selfish purposes lose it.

These stories and observations nearly always reveal one or more relationships that were important contributors to a beneficial outcome. Sometimes it appears within the researcher-community relationships, but more often (and more potently) it is a factor of the relationships that exist or which emerge within the community. Moreover, relationships seem to amplify the effects of the other factors mentioned here, and the influence is recursive, so that good relationships breed aspirations and accomplishment, which in turn generate good relationships.

The authors are led to conclude that evaluations will be less than satisfactory if they do not include consideration of these factors (probably others as well). Furthermore, the authors feel that the sustainability of an intervention cannot be assessed adequately unless all these factors are given due consideration. Of particular note is that these factors have their own dynamics, can come and go during the presence of the researchers, and will continue to exercise their influence in varying degrees over time after the researchers have left. Additionally, their net influence on outcomes is always, of course, the result of their interactions, so that any assessment of a single factor will not be complete until the others (and more) have been taken into consideration.

Finally, stories reveal more than the incident they describe. They imply the existence of their causalities, the strength or weakness of the social factors that brought them about. Moreover, they imply a set of possibilities, pointing to aspirations and capacity expansion, provoking remarks such as, "If they can do this...think what else might be possible." Stories therefore indicate much of their upstream precedents as well as their downstream prospects, divulging the richness of the social forces surrounding their formation.

This chapter is an examination of some of the experiences arising from two action research projects concerned with demonstrating the potential benefits of deploying ICTs within rural communities in developing countries by way of community telecenters. The focus of this chapter has been on lessons learned related to methodological issues for the practice in similar development interventions. As a young endeavor, telecenter practice and theory can benefit from aspects of methodological development in order to synthesize a body of knowledge for future application. The conclusions of this chapter concern two methodological aspects of telecenter implementation. They are requirements elicitation for implementing information systems and telecenter evaluation.

PAR provides an appropriate set of techniques that can be usefully incorporated into the community informatics approach to ICT use for rural communities in developing countries. Stories as evaluation contribute toward a rich understanding of the consequences of implementing rural community telecenters. PAR was not designed specifically for developing information systems within a community informatics informed approach to rural ICTs for development. Further methodological development will be required in order to narrow down the range of PAR activities and to refine them into more detailed actions that will be capable of achieving useful statements of information requirements in such settings.

Questions arise such as: "What form of participation works best?" "Who should participate and when?" "How should action and research interact?" Evidence from the examples suggests that the full realization of benefits from rural telecenters in developing countries takes a long time to emerge, sometimes many years. Consequently, requirements elicitation may have to stretch across the entire life of the implementation, as new uses evolve and as communities build their confidence with the technology. System design, therefore, cannot be considered complete at the time immediately prior to implementation.

Unlike more traditional approaches to design, system design becomes a continuous process with an indefinite end. This implies that participatory design techniques would be usefully incorporated into the processes of telecenter operations and management. Empowering communities with system design capability might be particularly challenging in the examples described previously. It also implies that design statements are naturally fluid, continually changing, even during system implementation, a challenge again for system developers.

Stories are anecdotal, but instead of searching for a better way to assemble numbers it might be preferable to seek out a better way of disclosing the truth. In accordance with the need for a methodological approach to stories, the methodology can provide guidance for at least the following activities:

- Story gathering
- Story verification
- Story recording
- Story interpretation
- Story dissemination
- Synthesis of story meanings

- Formation of conclusions
- Derivation of actions

Some of these activities may present challenges for information systems and development professionals who need to assess the impact of their rural telecenter activities. Gathering, verifying, and interpreting stories imply using skills that are derived from anthropological and ethnographic backgrounds. Disseminating and synthesizing stories might imply using photographic, video, and multimedia capabilities that might not be available. The IDRC has implemented several initiatives aimed at a better understanding of telecenter evaluation.

Among these, the PanAsia Telecenter Learning and Evaluation Group (PANTLEG), which consists of the three projects described here plus one in the Philippines and one in Mongolia, continues to explore and refine the use of stories as a means of evaluation. It is appropriate to assess the limitations of a participatory approach to system implementation methodologies for rural development and a stories-based form of outcome evaluation. The rural communities described here have no background in the use of computers. Often, experienced computer users find difficulty in articulating their information requirements from an information system that includes some new technology.

In many cases, it is difficult to conceive the uses of a technology whose capabilities are only vaguely understood. For most rural communities in Asia, ICTs are a completely new phenomenon about which they probably have no information that can guide them to its beneficial use. Under such circumstances, they will likely need skilful and sensitive guidance that allows for their participation where appropriate but which contextualizes it within a framework of possibilities for suitable use of ICTs. This implies a wide set of systems analysis skills additional to those already required, embracing the practice of community development as well as group facilitation.

Furthermore, the specificity of the communities described here implies that systems that are heavily based on participatory methods will produce solutions to problems that are highly local, hence limiting their scope and their impact. With regard to a stories-based form of outcome evaluation, there are limitations that relate to the absence of hard data and to the selectivity of stories. In many cases, however, evaluations tend to regard that which is tangible as substantial and that which is intangible as unsubstantial, whereas the opposite is often true.

While good stories can engage both the heart and the mind, the choice of which story to tell provides a potent lever for swinging the evaluation toward the storyteller's preferences. Balanced evaluations will reveal undesirable outcomes, primarily as learning opportunities, and should be augmented with hard data in order to satisfy the multiple stakeholder interests involved (e.g., donor agencies).

A full methodology for using stories for evaluation will ensure negative outcomes are exploited as learning opportunities, but such a methodology is yet to be articulated. Systems development methodologies have evolved in response to many challenges faced by systems professionals as technology has evolved, new users have taken up its use, and new applications have been found. In the latest development, ICTs are reaching the poorest of people and are having a profound effect on their lives.

The circumstances of such achievements present an entirely novel scenario to system developers, who are more accustomed to organizational settings, and to development practitioners, who are unfamiliar with the technology. New approaches are required to foster the blending of appropriate professional skills that will be needed for marginalized communities to enjoy the benefits of a wired world and for ICTs to realize their full potential for narrowing the digital divide.

4

The Social Context of Computing

One of the most important lessons we have learned through a century of psychological research is that people's behaviour, attitudes, and thoughts are impacted dramatically by the social context. To illustrate this point, we begin this chapter with a notorious incident that occurred many years ago in New York City. The incident and its aftermath led to a fascinating social psychological experiment that vividly drives home the important point: the social context matters. It shows how the simple presence of other people impacts a person's behaviour in dramatic and consequential ways.

In 1964, a woman named Kitty Genovese was attacked and stabbed multiple times over a 45-minute period on the street beneath her New York City apartment by an assailant with a knife. Investigations following her death indicated that although at least 38 people living in the apartment complex had either witnessed part of the attack or heard her screams and pleas for help, not one of them attempted to intervene or even call the police for assistance. Newspaper coverage following the case attributed the indifference of the neighbors to the fact that they were apathetic New Yorkers, desensitized to violence.

A social psychological study conducted after the Kitty Genovese attack, however, showed that the unresponsiveness of the neighbors may have been due not to apathy, but rather, in a sad twist of fate, to the fact that there were so many of them witnessing the attack. Following the Kitty Genovese murder, John Darley and Bibb Latane set out to investigate how the knowledge that others are present in an emergency situation may affect the degree to which each witness helps the victim.

In order to do this, they created a simulated emergency situation in a psychological laboratory at New York University. In their study, students were brought into the lab and were told that they would be talking with a group of other students about college life. Each of the students was seated in separate rooms, and was told that the discussion would be held via microphone in order to ensure the anonymity of the discussants. In fact, there was only one student who participated at a time, and the other "voices" were tape recordings designed to give the illusion that there were other people present in the study.

Because Darley and Latane were interested in investigating how the presence of other people influenced helping behaviour, they varied the number of others who were supposedly "present" in the other room. Some of the participants in their study were told that there was only one other student present, others were told that there were two others present, and a third group were told that there were five others present. In order to create a simulated emergency situation, shortly after the discussion began, a tape recording of one of the other "students" came on indicating that he was having an epileptic seizure. On the recording, the student asked for help and then the tape became silent.

Results from this study were dramatic. The number of people that participants thought was in the study greatly impacted whether each student individually took steps to provide assistance. More than 80% of the students who believed that they were alone with the student having the "seizure" immediately rose to help the other person. In contrast, only about 60% of those who believed that one other person was available to help provided immediate assistance, and, shockingly, only about 30% of those who thought that five others were present provided aid.

This study was important in showing that the mere presence of other people in a situation can have a large effect on how individuals in the situation will behave. Other psychological research has shown that the mere presence of other people can also influence people's task performance. This phenomenon is known as social facilitation. Studies on social facilitation have shown that under certain conditions, people show increased performance on some tasks when they perform them in front of an audience.

In the first study of this phenomenon, conducted more than a century ago, Triplett found that athletes, in this case bicycle riders, had faster racing times when they were racing as a group than when they were trying their best, but racing alone against a clock. Although the presence of an audience has been shown to increase performance on a wide variety of tasks such as typing, buying and selling in on-line auctions, and even performance at tug-of-war, other research has suggested that audiences do not always lead to increased performance.

Research since Triplett's study on bicycle racers has shown that the presence of other people increases performance only on tasks that performers are comfortable with those that are easy, well-rehearsed, and well-practiced. In contrast, the presence of an audience actually decreases people's performance on tasks that are anxiety-producing-those that are complicated and poorly learned. To illustrate this distinction, Michaels, Blommel, Brocato, Linkous, and Rowe examined how good and poor pool players performed when they were unaware they were being observed and when they were in front of an audience.

His study found that good pool players showed evidence of the social facilitation effect their performance increased when they were in front of an audience as compared to how they performed when they were not aware that they were being observed. Poor pool players, on the other hand, not only did not show the social facilitation effect, but actually showed the opposite. Because they were not comfortable with their pool skills, the poor players performed worse when in front of an audience than when they were under the impression that they were alone.

Just as we have seen that the social context can influence behaviour and performance in emergency situations and in task performance, the social context in which children perform computer tasks can have a large impact on how successful students are when performing computer tasks in the classroom. However, because few educators are aware of the degree to which social context factors influence performance, oftentimes classrooms are set up in such a way that exacerbates the problem rather than minimizing it.

This computer-based lesson will enable the children to see animated cartoon-like fish interact in a simulated aquatic environment. By manipulating the keys on their computers, they will be able to remove various elements of the fish's normal environment and learn of the consequences to the fish and marine life. The computer program is instructional and efficient. Its colorful display screen is a pleasure to behold.

If we reflect on the research on social facilitation, we know that the presence of others increases performance on well-learned tasks, and is detrimental to performance on poorly learned or anxiety-producing tasks. Females experience a high level of anxiety when they work with computer programs that have been designed with the features that are attractive to boys. In that chapter, we outlined several possible reasons for these gender differences in reactions to computers.

Because girls are less involved with video games as an extracurricular activity, they are not as used to or comfortable with the video game like "bells and whistles" that characterize many of the computer-assisted instructional programs being used in today's classrooms. Additionally, most computer tasks are male-oriented even beyond their video game-like qualities that is, they have many of the formal features that males prefer. Furthermore, societal stereotypes have imbued the field of computing with a reputation of being a generally male-oriented area. Females may also experience anxiety when attempting computer tasks because this reputation may lead them to have lower expectations for their own performance.

As a result of a combination of such factors, we know that

many females experience anxiety when working with computers. The research on social facilitation suggests that this anxiety will interact with the presence of others in a classroom. As a consequence, when computing in public, we can predict that girls, on average, will end up performing less well on school tasks that take place on the computer or the Internet. Boys, on the other hand, will not experience the same level of computer anxiety, and thus, when engaging in computer tasks, will not typically mind the presence of others.

In fact, similar to the way that expert pool players actually performed better when they were being watched by an audience, for boys who are comfortable with their computer skills, sometimes an audience may be the motivation they need to do a better job. The audience problem that affects girls and boys is of major importance and is multi-determined. Social facilitation is one of the social psychological factors that contribute to the gender difference. Psychological processes including complex stereotyping and expectancy confirmation converge on the same conclusion: When the social context for technological learning includes groups of children, the performance of girls is likely to suffer.

GENDER AND SOCIAL GROUPS

There is some irony to our suggestion that girls are uncomfortable computing in the presence of others. Typically, females are much more comfortable in groups than are males. Anyone who has had the opportunity to observe teenagers, for example, knows that teenage girls tend to have more expansive social groups than teenage boys, are more expressive and compassionate with their comrades, and prefer the company of others. Ample research has corroborated these observations. It is also true that girls tend to do quite well in so-called "cooperative learning tasks" where the outcome of a lesson depends on the cooperation and communication among peers.

So, it is not that females shun social groupings or are less comfortable in the presence of others. To the contrary, computing in the presence of other people may make more anxious despite her general proclivity to enjoy social groups. The irony of computer anxiety is that it is manifested in a public context if, and only if, the computing task is one that provokes anxiety in the first place. As we noted at the beginning of this chapter, social facilitation, or the fact that audiences increase performance on tasks on which people feel comfortable and decrease performance on tasks on which people feel anxious or uncomfortable, is a very basic psychological finding. Currently, for girls and women, it is typically the case that the presence of others will inhibit their performance.

SHEDDING LIGHT ON THE THEORY

The research we examine first was conducted in the United Kingdom with 11-and 12-year-old boys and girls. The children participated in a very cute IT task in which they needed to help a group of partying honey bears solve a logistical problem. In the "Honeybears" task, originally devised by Littleton, Light, Joiner, Messer, and Barnes, the children's goal is to find a route by which the teddy bears, who were picnicking at Almwood, could recover the honey that they had left at Flint without its falling prey to the Honeymonsters.

As the children progress in the task, they learn that Honeymonsters steal honey from any boat crossing the river, so a new way has to be found to get it across the river. The children have to find the proper solution, which is to transport the Honeybears to Flint via balloon. The children must discover the hidden information that leads to the balloon solution, while also learning about the system's constraints (e.g., how the bears move, how many can move, how the boats move, and so forth).

The Honeybears task is such that progress toward the ultimate goal can be measured numerically. The more information the children discovered, the higher their score. The closer they came to bringing the honey back to Almwood, the higher their score. Performance was measured on a scale ranging from zero (the children failed to make any move) to 6 (the children found the honey and brought it all the way back, without complication from the Honeymonsters.

Children played this adorable game in groups of two. Each child had a computer, each could see the other working, but each person worked at his or her own machine and each had his or her progress measured separately. In half of the cases, the two children were of the same sex. In the other half, the children were of the opposite sex. How well did they perform?

The results of Light *et al.* (2000) experiment showed clearly that the boys who worked in two-person dyads outperformed girls. Boys significantly outperformed girls on the Honeybears task. The second question that Light et al. asked is whether children would be more or less affected by being in single-sex or mixed-sex groups. Presumably, all children would experience greater anxiety in the presence of an 11- or 12-year-old of the opposite sex. This should lead to greater social facilitation. For girls, this should mean more anxiety, and less positive performance.

For boys, this should mean greater challenge and motivation to get the right answer quickly on this computerized adventure game. This is precisely what happened. Boys showed improved performance in mixed-sex groups, whereas girls who computed in mixed-sex groups showed the poorest performance of all. The statistical interaction was significant. Whether Jared and Martha are learning reading in kindergarten, guiding Honeybears on their adventures in the sixth grade, or learning biology in the ninth grade, Martha will have a problem when working on IT software in public.

In those rare cases in which their teachers find software that has the formal features girls adore and boys shun, then computing in public may cause boys to show performance decrements and girls to show better performance. But in the usual cases, where the IT software has the formal features that boys prefer, the boys will prosper when computing in the presence of others. The girls will not be so fortunate. They will experience computer anxiety and stress. They will also learn less from their teacher's well-intentioned computer lessons.

DEMOLITION DIVISION

We presented research showing that girls experienced greater anxiety than boys when learning from Demolition Division, and that boys experienced greater anxiety than girls when learning with Arithmetic Classroom. We now re-examine those conclusions in light of the current discussion. Let's look more closely at that research. What was the social milieu in which the computing was conducted?

Indeed, the data presented came from students who used computers in a public room. Recall that we found that, when students used the computer program that was male-oriented, girls experienced far more anxiety than did boys. Demolition Division's fast paced competitive action within a war game metaphor raised the anxiety level for the sixth-grade girls. Conversely, the verbal feedback emphasis of the Arithmetic Classroom program caused stress and anxiety for the boys. The results of this research came exclusively from children who performed the computer-assisted instruction task in a public context.

Let's visualize the look of the computer room. Each child sat in front of a computer screen. To his or her left and right were other children with the same assignment and provided with similar computers. Most were intent on their computer task; others milled about. The situation was probably fraught with less social anxiety than Light *et al.* (2000) study because the only children present were of the same gender. Girls were brought to the computer room without any boys present; similarly, boys only worked on their programs in the presence of other boys.

They were given the same instructions, tested for their ability at solving division problems and were given the Mattson Anxiety Scale. The only difference between children in this "alone" condition and the children (those in the "others present" condition) is that these children came to a computer in a school room without any other children present. Each boy or girl faced Demolition Division or Arithmetic Classroom on his or her computer without any child or adult present. Did it make a difference? The answer is a resounding yes.

There are no meaningful differences between the anxiety levels expressed by boys and by girls when they used the program by themselves. As in the data we looked at before, Demolition Division is a more stressful exercise than Arithmetic Classroom. The quick pace of the competition, the demand for eye-hand coordination, and the exploding tanks or canons yielded higher stress scores for everyone. However, the differences between males and females that were so dramatic when the children worked in the presence of others is completely absent from the current data.

Taken together, the results take the form of a three-way statistical interaction. Anxiety is predicted by a combination of three variables: the gender of the learner, the formal features of the program, and the context in which the children did their computing. We saw the importance of two of these variables. Males experience anxiety when working with a computer program that has the formal features preferred by females. Females experience anxiety when working with a program containing the formal features preferred by males. To this we can now add the qualification: when using the computer in the presence of others.

What is it that bothers people about computing in public? As briefly mentioned before, there are many reasons that the presence of others might increase anxiety. Perhaps people worry about competition. If girls expect that they will not do well at a computer game, then they may be more worried than boys about the outcome of the competition. If Martha looks at the format of Demolition Division, she may anticipate that she will not do well at this boy-oriented game whose metaphor is war and destruction, and whose format requires so many of the activities that she would rather avoid.

Martha may or may not consciously reason that boys will outperform girls on this task. In fact, when Light and his colleagues asked their U. K. children whether boys or girls are better at computer tasks, one third of the children of each gender said it was the boys. Not a single boy nor a single girl indicated that girls are better at computer tasks.

THE PROBLEM OF COMPETITION

Many school environments are notorious for their reliance on competition. The desire to out-perform one's peers is often used to motivate students to reach the peak of their performance. For older children, classroom grades, academic advancement, and admission to higher education all rely on one's academic standing relative to other children. As we have suggested, girls like Martha have been given an abundance of reasons to believe that they will not do as well as boys in IT competition. The mere fact that Martha knows that learning a lesson on a computer is not a task at which she is likely to do well is sufficient to be both demoralizing and anxiety arousing. We should not be surprised that these emotions alone will lead to poorer performance on an IT task.

The results of empirical studies confirm the deleterious effects of group competition on girls' performance on IT tasks. Imagine three broad types of structured computer lessons in the classroom. One may be called individualistic and calls for students to take turns performing the activity, with evaluation focused on the individual student's performance. A second may be cooperative, in that students perform tasks in groups, and the achievement of one group member is linked to that of his or her fellow group member. If one member of the group performs well, the other members benefit. A third structure is competitive. In this group structure, if one group member performs well in competitive learning situations, the other group members will fare more poorly by comparison.

The effect of individualistic, cooperative, and competitive learning environments was studied by Johnson, Johnson, andStanne (1985). Intheirresearch, eighth-grade students learned geography using an interesting IT simulation. They learned to use the positions of the stars, the position of the sun, ocean depth, climate, and trade winds to navigate an ancient ship to a new continent in search of gold. Learning the daily geography lessons made it possible for the students to overcome obstacles (such as being stranded at sea or being attacked by pirates) that the computer program put in their paths. Thus, once again, an adventure metaphor subtly reminded the students that the task was one that communicated to boys more than to girls.

In their study, Johnson and his colleagues randomly placed students in an individualistic learning condition, a cooperative learning condition, or a competitive learning condition. Students in the cooperative condition were placed in four-person, gender-balanced groups and were given roles to play (e.g., captain, meteorologist) that helped them share their knowledge with each other. They were to be given individual daily quizzes and an individual final test to assess their knowledge, but they were told that their grade on the unit would be calculated by averaging the individual scores of each of the members of their group. Therefore, it was to each person's advantage that everyone else in the group learns their information and performs well on the exams.

In the competitive condition, students were also placed in gender-balanced groups of four children, but the rules were different. Students in the competitive condition were told that their final grades would be based on how they performed relative to the other members of their group and that they would receive bonus points for finishing before other students in the class. Students in the individual condition were simply told that they would complete the quizzes and the final alone and that they should do their own work.

The results of the quizzes and final exam showed that the structure of the computer learning environment made an important difference in students' learning. Students in the competitive condition learned significantly less geography and performed more poorly on the IT task than students in the individualistic or cooperative conditions. Students in the cooperative learning condition performed best.

The effect of group structure in Johnson et al.'s study was more important for girls than it was for boys. Girls performed just as well as boys in the individualistic and the cooperative learning conditions. Competitive instructions, however, had a particularly detrimental effect on the girls. They learned less geography and scored more poorly on the daily quizzes and final exams than did the boys. Although having to compete with peers in the technology lesson affected everyone, it hurt the girls the most.

In fact, the competitive environment had wide ranging and invidious effects that went beyond girls' reduced mastery of geography. In a follow-up survey, girls who had been in the competitive condition reported that they liked geography less than did the other children in the classroom, including the boys who had also been in the competitive condition. Moreover, the girls in the competitively structured groups felt that they had received less support from their learning environment, perceiving the teacher as insufficiently helpful.

Girls in the competitive condition also reported liking computers less and reported that they were less confident in their ability to use computers than were their male counterparts. Recall that children were assigned to their learning condition at random. There were no systematic differences in knowledge or attitudes prior to their being placed in one of the three learning environments. This forces us to conclude that being in a competitive group environment for their geography lessons caused girls to learn less and also caused them to feel negatively about their own ability at computers, forming more negative attitudes toward information technology in the process.

OTHER EFFECTS OF THE SOCIAL CONTEXT

Why else might a girl in Ms. Martin's class experience anxiety? Perhaps it is not only competition per se, but just the knowledge of how she compares to her classmates that is upsetting. If Martha's friend is also performing the biology exercise, looking at each other perform can provide knowledge of how each of them stacks up against the other, and this might be the cause of stress.

This is not competition in the sense of their being some clear standard for who "wins" or whether there is a reward for good performance. Rather, it is the knowledge of where one stands relative to others that can be both informative and potentially upsetting. If Martha sees her friend working away at the task or if she believes that her friend is observing or overhearing Martha work on the task, then stress and anxiety may occur for both of them. In the male-oriented biology program, or in Demolition Division, neither Martha nor her friend will likely feel optimistic about their performances and each may expect the results of the social comparison to be stressful.

A still simpler version of why public contexts are stressful is the mere knowledge that someone else will know how you did at a task. Especially when the task is one at which you do not expect to do well, then the mere knowledge that someone else knows how you are doing may cause anxiety. In this version of a public context, it is not necessary for a person to be competing with another for a reward, nor there any question of who is better or worse at a particular task. In this version, some other person's knowledge of how well you performed may be sufficient to arouse anxiety. We investigate this question in the next section.

MEN AND WOMEN PLAY ZORK

Zork was an ideal computer task for research purposes. In a manner similar to Honeybears, the game has a specific goal, and people's progress toward the goal can be measured. Therefore, we could not only find out if playing the computer game created anxiety under specific, predictable circumstances, but we could also measure the degree of success people had.

Our students volunteered to play Zork as a part of a research study. We told them about the game, and then brought them to the room in which the computer was located. They needed only a few words of instructions to begin the game. Because the adventure format of Zork made it the kind of game that has the formal features the males like, we predicted that the women in our study would experience anxiety and that their performance would not be as successful as males.

But what of the social context? Does it matter whether the students engaged in the Zork task alone or in the presence of others? The results of our study with middle school children already demonstrated that anxiety is manifested only in the social or public context. Would the same phenomenon happen with older students? Our prediction was that it would-that computer anxiety would occur primarily or perhaps only, in the presence of other people.

This prediction still leaves us in a quandary about what we mean by the term "other people around." Specifically, we were interested in looking at what it is about the public nature of the computing context that causes the expression of anxiety at a cross-gender task. We have discussed three possibilities that may make a public context conducive to experience anxiety. First, there was competition-expecting that you will lose to other people who are also performing the task. Second, there was social comparison-the knowledge that you and others may acquire about where you stack up among people in your group. Third, there was mere knowledge-the cognition that some other person or persons will know how you performed. Each of these may create anxiety if the nature of the computer task is one that communicates that it is a task at which you are not expected to do very well.

For the other three possible representations of public context in the mind of an individual, there had to be some reasonable complexity in the structure of the social context. People needed to be performing the same task. They had to have knowledge of each other's performance and needed some way to interpret the meaning either of the final product of the computing or a way to interpret the meaning of what was on each other's computer screen.

All of these complexities are reasonable in most computing situations. They were likely to have been present when Martha, Jared and their classmates set out to work on Ms. Martins' biology program. All of these possibilities existed when British sixth-grade children in the study by Light et al. (2000) and American sixth-grade children in the study by Cooper et al. (1990) computed in the public condition at their middle schools.

In this study, to begin with the simplest of all meanings of "public" context-what might call "mere presence?" Our hypothesis is that in a male-oriented adventure game, women will experience computer anxiety just because someone else is present in a room. If eliminate competition, if we eliminate knowledge of the other's performance, and any other complicating factor, the mere presence of another person will still foment anxiety in the computer user.

When a university student agreed to play Zork in our study, we ushered him or her to the room in which the computer was set up to play the game. For half of the participants, there was no one else in the room and he or she proceeded to begin the game. For the other half of the participants, another person was already seated at the far end of the room, working on a computer. The researcher indicated to the participant that the computer that was vacant was the computer on which Zork was loaded. The researcher also apologized that the research team could not locate a room in which there was only a single computer.

It is advisable to have the confederate of the same gender as the research participant. Although it is surely interesting in its own right, we did not want to complicate the effects of the presence of other people with social concerns in a mixed-gender situation. In the public condition, therefore, the letter-writing confederate was male if the participant was male, female if the participant was female. After each participant played Zork for 30 minutes, we asked him or her to stop. Following the game, each participant was given a battery of questionnaires including an adult version of the Mattson anxiety questionnaire that we used in the research.

The computer automatically tracked each player's progress toward the goal, which gave us a measure of performance to complement the anxiety measure. Zork is a male-oriented computer game. Did females experience anxiety? The results of the Mattson anxiety measure show that they did-but only if they computed in the presence of another person. Look at the anxiety that our participants. It shows that, when another person was present, women reported considerably more anxiety than men (mean scores of 4.6 for females vs. 3.3 for males). However, when they computed in private, there was no meaningful difference in reported anxiety (means of 3.7 and 3.9 for women and men, respectively).

Now let's look at performance scores. How well did male and female college students do at solving the computer task presented by Zork? Once again, the social context was critical. When working alone, female students outperformed male students by a wide margin. The score for male students averaged 6.7. The average score for females was 19.1. However, when another person was present, the data completely turned around. This time, males' performance scores soared to 16.3, while the score for females plummeted to 1.4.

These data teach that women can perform as well as men on the computer task. In fact, for this particular task, they can perform a great deal better-provided that they compute in a private context. Perhaps our female participants were more adept at this task; perhaps they were more motivated than the male students for this particular task. Either way, they showed their ability to succeed at Zork as long as they were alone. However, in the presence of another student even though that other student was the same gender as the participant and was doing something completely different from the Zork game and paying no apparent attention to the Zork player the female participants experienced great anxiety, and their performance collapsed.

By contrast, males seemed to rise to whatever challenge the presence of another person created. With the confederate present, males kept their anxiety in check and achieved significantly higher scores. The data also offer a glimpse at how the differences in anxiety turned into differences in performance scores. In the presence of other people, female college students were more anxious and achieved lower scores on the computer task. The computer was able to record another statistic that we have labeled "Actions."

An action is an attempt to do something in response to a dilemma posed by the Zork adventure. For example, if the computer wrote to a player indicating that there was a monster located to the east and north of the player, one action might be to turn the protagonist's character to the south. This may turn out to be a productive action on the player's part, allowing him or her to avoid a confrontation and make progress toward the goal. Alternatively, the player may choose to turn north. This would not be a productive action because it would result in an altercation that would, at the very least, allow valuable minutes to go by without making progress toward finding the treasure.

A second alternative might be for a player to sit at his or her computer, unsure of which action to take and, consequently, do nothing. The first two courses are considered "actions" because the player took measures to solve the dilemma. Even though only one of the choices was correct, both would be scored similarly as actions. Only the second alternative, doing nothing, would be scored differently because no action was taken.

How did our research participants do? The data presented show clear and significant differences on the "action" measure. When alone, both males and females took a moderate number of actions in response to their dilemmas (6.7 and 7.0, respectively). The difference between these numbers is trivial and not statistically significant. On the other hand, males working with Zork in the presence of others not only had their anxiety reduced, but also raised the number of actions to a mean of 13.0. Females working in the presence of others had their anxiety level raised and, they took very few actions.

Their mean number of actions fell to 4.1. Thus, in the presence of other people, the picture for female players in this male-oriented action game was to experience significantly greater stress than males or than females who worked on the game alone. Their response was to lower their output that is, to stop trying. They took very few right or wrong actions and, as a result, their scores plummeted. Males, whose performance was mediocre at best when playing alone, lowered their anxiety in public performances. They responded by trying lots of things, some of them right and some of them wrong. But the act of trying allowed them to find enough correct solutions to their dilemmas to raise their final performance scores.

In Allentown, Pennsylvania, Judy Lichtman (1998) observed the way middle-school girls and boys behaved on computers. Her observations correspond to our findings. She observed, "When girls do sit down at a computer, they tend to wait for instructions and blame themselves when something doesn't work. In contrast, boys often approach technology with an aggressive, experimental attitude; clicking their way to a solution. Boys develop confidence which comes from an intimate knowledge and mastery of technology".

Thus, research shows that the social context makes a huge difference in how well people use the computer and how comfortable they are while doing it. Public performances seem to result in anxiety for people using computer programs that are primarily designed for the other gender. Yet, these effects occurred even when the public nature of the performance was minimal indeed. In our study, there was no communication between the computer user and the person sharing his or her room. There was no opportunity for competition or social comparison, nor was there any chance the stranger in the room could have knowledge of the student's performance.

It almost seems that the mere presence of another person magically transformed men into high computer achievers and women into highly anxious users with limited achievement. We would imagine that, as in the laboratory of Light et al. (2000), these effects would only be exacerbated in situations in which the girls and boys actually felt like their peers or others were watching them, measuring them, and gauging how well they did on the computer task.

Anxiety is both a cause and an effect of boys' and girls' different levels of performance at the computer. Because anxiety interferes with complex learning, it drives down girls' level of accomplishment. With repeated exposures, the mere thought of having to work at a computer creates a further expectation of relative failure, which, in turn, increases the level of anxiety and stress. The cycle almost certainly continues, and grows more automatic with repeated occurrences. In the Robinson-Stavely and Cooper (1990) research, we conducted a second experiment that was designed to provide one way to break the cycle.

For reasons we have already discussed, girls expect that they will not do well at computational tasks, especially when they perform those tasks in the presence of others. Boys expect otherwise. Relative to girls, they have confidence in their ability to take on computational tasks and are even more determined to show it in the presence of others. Boys' expectations arouse confidence that leads to heightened performance. Girls' expectations beget anxiety, which, in turn, produces poorer performance at the computer.

In our second study, we wondered what would happen if we changed girls' expectations and cause them to anticipate that they would be superb at using the computer. For practical reasons, we thought that it was too tall an order to change anyone's estimation of their overall ability in a field of endeavor in one experimental session. (The current authors know, for example, that if we were told that we should expect to play chess like chess masters, it would be a very tough sell indeed!) On the other hand, it might be possible to convince someone that she will do very well at a particular computer task, regardless of how well or poorly she may have done with information technology in the past.

Robinson-Stavely and Cooper's second study again featured Princeton University students playing the game of Zork. As in the first experiment (reported earlier), half of the males and half of the females played Zork alone; the other half played with the mere coexistence of someone else in the room. In the second experiment, however, we systematically manipulated males and females expectations of how successful they will be at Zork. Before starting the game, each student was seated alone at a computer and filled out what appeared to be a psychological survey assessing their personal characteristics and prior experiences.

When they were finished, the computer automatically "scored" their questionnaire and provided them with feedback about how they could expect to do at the Zork task. Unbeknownst to the participants, the feedback was actually written by the experimenters and came in one of two versions. In the "Expect Success" condition, the feedback stated, "The test results from your interest and personality inventory tell us that you will do very well at the game of Zork. Your profile matches the types of skills required by the task. Regardless of how you have done in the past at computer tasks, you should expect to do very well at this game. "

Students in the "Expect Failure" condition were provided with less optimistic news. They were told, "The test results from your interest and personality inventory tell us that you will probably not do very well at the game of Zork. Your profile shows skills and interests that may interfere with successful performance. Regardless of how you have done in the past at computer tasks, you should not expect to do very well at this game. "

Following the feedback, students were given a description of the Zork game. After reading about the game, they were given a short survey that included a crucial question about how they expected to do at the game of Zork. Most participants responded to the crucial question in a way that indicated they believed the manipulation. Regardless of their overall skill level at computers, they came to expect that, on this particular task, they would do well or poorly, depending on the feedback that they had received from their personality and interest test.

Of course, not everyone believed the manipulation, and it is informative to look at who did and who did not believe the feedback. When students were told that they probably would not do well, 19 out of 20 women believed the manipulation. Men believed it, too, with 17 out of 20 indicating that they did not expect to do well. What is particularly interesting is the result in the positive expectancy condition. Men tended to believe the manipulation, with 74% (14 out of 19) expecting to succeed. When women were told to expect success at Zork, the percentage who believed the manipulation dropped to 55%. Nine of the 20 women thought that they would not be able to do well at Zork.

Nonetheless, when we examined the performance of our university students at the Zork game, we saw evidence of the pattern we had predicted. Considering only the students who believed our manipulation, we found that students who were led to believe they would be successful were more successful than students who expected to fail. As we predicted, this was mostly true when the computing was done in the presence of others. Furthermore, it was equally true of both sexes.

Men and women who expected to fail showed a pattern of results just like the pattern that women showed in the first experiment. Men and women who expected to succeed showed a pattern just like the men's pattern in the first experiment. In other words, when women's previously learned tendency to think they would not do well was overridden by our specific instruction that they could expect to excel at this particular task, then they performed quite well. And, consistent with our analysis of the stress-arousing nature of the presence of others, these results occurred only in the public context.

When expecting success in the public context, students achieved a score of 17.4, the highest of all of the scores. When expecting failure in a public context, they scored only 11.3, the lowest achievement of all of the conditions. Computing in private produced scores in the mid-range (15.0 and 12.1) was not statistically different from one another. When students were asked about their level of stress, they showed the predicted response. For men and women, the level of stress and general anxiety was highest when computing in the presence of other people while under the burden of expecting to fail.

Our conclusion from this series of studies sounds both a pessimistic and an optimistic note. The pessimistic note is that people who feel they will not perform well at a computer task are under a special burden. Although they can cope with their expectation of failure while performing alone, they cannot overcome their burden in the presence of others. Anxiety and stress overwhelm them and interfere with their success. Performance tumbles, which probably undermines future expectations and enhances future levels of stress.

The first study in the Robinson-Stavely and Cooper (1990) series shows that stress and computer anxiety resides most heavily in women and it is they who suffer in the presence of others. By contrast, the second study sounds the optimistic note. When given a believable expectation that they will succeed at an IT task, women perform just as well as men. They do not report anxiety and they are not troubled by the social context. We should be able to build upon this result to help level the computer playing field for men and women.

SOCIAL CONTEXT AFFECTS SOCIAL COGNITION

The social context of computing affects what people think as well as what they feel. To this point, we have highlighted the impact of the social context on children's motivations and emotions. Anxiety and stress dominate the performance of girls when they use IT programs in public, whereas boys seem to become more enthused, eager, and productive while computing in the public arena. There are also changes in what boys and girls think and remember when they compute in a public context, especially in mixed-sex groups.

Recall that, in a number of surveys, boys reported that they were more experienced with computers than were girls. Girls reported having negative attitudes toward computers and a higher degree of stress. Let's focus, though, on the survey results that show that girls report having less experience on the computer and having fewer computers in their homes than do the boys. There are two possibilities to ponder. One is the obvious explanation, and it is likely to be true. Families are less likely to purchase computers for their daughters than for their sons, and girls are less likely to use their computers than are boys. We do not doubt that these recollections are based on reality, but does it completely account for the finding?

There is a second possibility that may amplify the differences between girls' and boys' memories of the availability and use of computers. It is possible that the social context exaggerates, and perhaps sometimes actually causes, the differences in the way boys and girls think about and remember their experiences with information technology. Girls and boys may retrospectively distort their level of computer experience in gender stereotypic ways.

The other groups were either all boys or all girls. When girls filled out the survey in mixed-sex groups, they reported that they spent less time each day on the computer than did the girls who filled out the survey in a group with other girls. Precisely the opposite pattern was found for boys. When boys filled out the questionnaire in a mixed-sex group, they reported spending more time on the computer than when they responded in groups made up only of boys. In mixed company, boys and girls conformed to the stereotype of what is expected of people of their sex.

The result would surprise if the students answered in public. Boys may be motivated to start their computer-literate feathers in front of the girls in their group, while girls may want to make a public show of shunning this boy-friendly technology. However, the middle school students in the Cooper and Stone study were reporting their computer-related judgments on a confidential questionnaire. Why did the girls report spending less time with IT when boys were present? Why did boys recall spending more time with computers when girls were present? We can only speculate about the process, but we believe the social context may produce cognitive distortions-that is, errors in the way people perceive and recall events in their environment.

It is likely that the presence of youngsters of the opposite sex causes boys and girls to think of themselves in terms of their gender. We examine examples of this phenomenon when a solo member of one sex finds himself or herself in a group comprised exclusively of members of the other sex. Research on this phenomenon, often referred to as tokenism, shows the deleterious impact on people's cognitive abilities when they are solo representatives of their gender group.

However, even when boys and girls are not solo members of their groups, the mere presence of the other group highlights their membership in a gender group. Thus, boys think of themselves more as boys, girls think of themselves more as girls, when the groups are of mixed gender. When a girl thinks of herself as a girl, she is "primed" to think of behaviours and thoughts that are consistent with what she thinks is stereotypical of girls. It is not that she wants to lie about her computer use.

Rather, when primed with the category of her gender, she is more likely to scan her memory for recollections consistent with her identity as a girl. Similarly, boys scan their memories for cognitions consistent with what boys stereotypically do and think. The boy, when his gender is highlighted, may recall his participation in sports, his interest in science, or his last trip to the video arcade. When asked about computer use, he vividly recalls the hours or minutes that he spent in front of the computer, playing games, doing homework, or surfing the Web.

When the girl has her gender highlighted, she is more likely to remember her conversations with her friends and less likely to remember the time spent at the computer screen. In this way, just being in a group of boys and girls makes each person recall thoughts that are consistent with his or her gender stereotype. The boy exaggerates his recollection of his computer use and, by extension, his interest in information technology. The girl underrepresents her activity at the computer and, by extension, infers she has less interest in IT.

SEX COMPOSITION OF COMPUTER CLASSES

Not only does the social context of computing influence students' retrospective memories for the amount of time they spend on the computer, it also reminds them of society's expectations for their gender. A common theme that arose in many of our interviews with Princeton University freshmen was that there are pronounced gender differences in the number of boys and girls taking computer classes, advanced mathematics classes, and advanced physics classes in the high schools they attended. Our female students thought that the unequal gender distribution was detrimental in a variety of ways.

Karen, a student who had attended a public high school in Southern California, remembered, "There were about six girls in my AP Physics class as compared to about 34 guys. When I looked around at the students in the class, the societal belief that guys are better at this than girls came to my mind. I tried to tell myself that it was no big deal, that I can do this too. " Karen continued, "We know that stereotypes are out there and we know that other students might feel a certain way. Maybe this unconsciously affects us. "

Monica, a student who attended a public high school in Chicago, had a similar story: "I was the only girl in my physics class with eight boys. The first couple of weeks I felt very intimidated. " Women are also affected by the stories their friends tell them. Susan's best friend was the only female in an advanced math class in high school: "My friend used to tell me that she felt like she did not fit in. She would sit in the corner of the classroom and not talk to anyone. I wasn't very interested in taking that class. "

Not only did our female students notice the gender disparity in many upper level math and science courses, some of the male students noticed it too. Elliot, a student from Atlanta offered, "The makeup of my math classes and computer classes was 70-80% male on average. Most of the girls, even if they were capable of the work, were turned off by the lack of females in the course. " Gender divides in course composition can influence students' perceptions in many different ways.

Courses with unequal numbers of girls and boys may make stereotypes salient, and may send a message to girls and young women that the topic of study is not for them or people like them. Karen, for instance, had to remind herself several times that she too could do the work in physics. Teachers in these courses, who are overwhelmingly male, also may take a demonstrative male majority as an opportunity to gear the examples toward the male audience.

Using examples such as sports statistics in math and computer classes can be alienating for the girls present, especially if they do not understand the relationships between the teams, the meaning of sports terminology, and so on. Like Denise, one of our female students remembered this happening in her computer class in high school: "One teacher used a lot of sports examples, specifically the Celtics. But that's because he was a sports fanatic you should've seen the guy's office! But I like sports so that wasn't a problem for me. But I can see how other girls might have felt unincluded in some class conversations because of it. "

Although this young woman was not bothered by the sports examples herself, one can easily see how it may turn off other girls and even make a course more difficult for girls. For instance, if batting average is used as a computer example, not knowing what it is makes the example more confusing and difficult to understand, above and beyond an already intimidating computer programming assignment.

In addition to making societal stereotypes salient, when the classroom social context skewed in favour of more boys, this can also inadvertently help confirm gender stereotypes. That is, when there are more boys than girls in a class, often the best student in the class is a boy. Students may see this as confirmation of the societal stereotypes, that boys are better at computers or math than girls. However, given the different base rates of boys and girls in the classes, it is more likely a consequence of the numbers. For instance, Karen noted that boys seemed to do better than girls in her physics class that had about 85% boys and 15% girls.

When asked to explain why she thought the boys were better than the girls, she talked about research showing that boys have superior spatial relationships skills than girls. However, a more subtle and perhaps accurate reason might have simply been because there were 34 boys and 6 girls in the class, thus making it more probable that the top student would be a boy.

INTERACTIONS BETWEEN BOYS AND GIRLS IN UNEQUAL CLASSROOMS

The students' stories also made it clear that gender disparities in courses can also lead to detrimental social dynamics between the majority group of boys and the minority group of girls. Nicole, a student from Virginia, for instance, was the only girl on her school's "Academic Team," a selective team that competed with other high schools on academic exercises. Nicole remembered that being the only girl was difficult and intimidating at times, and recalled that "the boys on the team used to make jokes about boys being smarter. I always pretended to laugh along with them at the jokes, but inside it really bothered me and even sometimes made me angry. I was the focus of attention and it was awkward. I wondered why they kept saying it when it really was not that funny at all. "

In addition to facing what are essentially sexist jokes, some of our male students pointed out other social dynamics they saw in the classrooms. In particular, the male students remembered that young women in their courses often looked up to the young men for help on assignments and class projects. Lyle, a student from Connecticut who planned to major in molecular biology at Princeton, noted that, "In my higher math classes, the other males, but especially the females, looked to guys to know and solve every problem known to man. "

Other young men noted similar dynamics in their courses. Steven, for instance, pointed out, "males were treated better [in advanced math and science courses] because the course seemed very male oriented. It is a common stereotype that engineers are males, and that the engineering field is geared toward males. Most of the males stuck it out just because they were males and they were expected to be better. " Others mirrored these comments. Greg mentioned, for instance, "Girls always assumed guys knew more so they would ask them for help."

Interestingly, at least one young woman had a difference recollection about whether girls were more likely to ask boys for help on assignments. Maria, for instance, remembered, "I noticed that several of the males in the class seemed to think it was their responsibility to help me if I was ever stuck or confused about something while we were in the computer lab writing programs. I preferred going to the teacher for help, though. "

We see that the social context plays a very crucial role in encouraging or discouraging children's and adults' success with the computer. Our search of the literature finds very few differences in males' and females' competence with the computer, when they are using information technology by themselves. As soon as computing becomes public, however, the arrangement of the social context can make an enormous difference in the way people feel and think. Computer anxiety becomes exacerbated in public. Girls and boys become more motivated to conform to their social stereotypes, to the detriment of the girls' performance on the computer. Overall, males expect to succeed; girls worry about failing. Girls think of themselves as less computer literate and recall far fewer successful experiences on the computer than do boys.

As we have seen, the gender composition of children's groups when learning or performing an IT task plays a very important role in how children feel and think about themselves. However, the mere presence of others - even of the same gender - produces deleterious effects on girls' achievement. Nor do adults escape the invidious role played by the social group. Women continue to perform more poorly when computing in a social context.

It is not likely that public or private schools will be able to provide individual instruction in computing technology any time soon. One reason is that there are some very sound pedagogical advantages for group instruction across the school curriculum. Another reason is financial. Spending on IT in schools in the United States reached $6.5 billion in 1998-1999, achieving a computer-to-student ratio of 1 to 16. The cost to taxpayers of achieving a 1-to-1 ratio will be staggering. The question we will need to deal with, as educators and as members of society, is how to change the social context into a powerful instrument to create, rather than to undermine, equal opportunity and equal achievement.

5

The Problem and the Solution

In the last two decades, computers have proliferated in classrooms the world over. In 1981, for example, fewer than 20% of school classrooms in the world had computers. By the end of that decade, more than 95% of all classrooms had at least one computer. By the year 2000, virtually all schools owned computers, and 98% were connected to the Internet.

The rate at which schools have been purchasing computers has been climbing at greater than 10% per year, with purchases running at approximately $1 billion annually. Unquestionably, computers are becoming a central feature of education from kindergarten to college and beyond.

To the casual observer, computers in classrooms may be impressive. But discerning critics, be they parents, teachers or researchers, must look beyond colored screens, sound effects, and moving icons. What can computers teach children? Do computers motivate children to learn more than traditional instructional methods? Has the computer affected children's ability to think in different ways? Does introducing the computer at young ages prepare children better for the workplace of the future?

Computers can add constructively to the educational process both through educational programs designed to motivate children to learn material from traditional disciplines, and also by the inclusion of the computer as a topic of study itself in fields like computer science.

RACE, WEALTH, AND THE DIGITAL DIVIDE

Education and the workplace have been revolutionized by information technology. The jobs of tomorrow will depend heavily on people's literacy with computers and the Internet. Forecasts are that by the year 2010, 25% of all of the new jobs created in the private and public sectors will be "technologically oriented".

In both economic upturns and downturns, access to jobs will require training and competency in technology. Yet, access to training in IT is not equitable and some people have greater access than others with the likelihood depending on the income, racial, and gender categories of which people are members. White Americans are more likely to have access to computers and the Internet than African Americans. Males have more access than females, and wealthier Americans have more access regardless of race and gender.

The digital divide is a term that has been used to refer to the gap between those who have access to technology and those who do not; between those who have the expertise and training to utilize technology and those who do not. According to Chistopher Latimer in a report to the New York State Forum for Information Resources, social gaps in society cause the digital divide, but the digital divide, in turn, may intensify existing social gaps and create new ones. Because members of minority groups and people from lower socioeconomic groups have less access to technology, they are likely to be even further disadvantaged from attaining some of the higher positions in tomorrow's economy, widening the economic divisions that already exist.

The trend is already occurring. According to a report of the National Science Foundation, 46.6% of White families in the United States own a home computer, whereas only 23.2% of African American families own one. Although computer purchase and use rose for both Whites and Blacks over the last several years, the gap between racial groups has widened. During the 4-year period of 1994-1998, Papadakis reported that computer ownership increased 18% nationally, but the gap between Blacks and Whites widened by an additional 7%.

The gap seems to persist at the college level. For instance, the Office of Institutional Research at a community college in northern Virginia polled the commuter-oriented student population and, even among this group, computer ownership was higher among White students than it was among Black students. Socioeconomic status also plays a large role. Of Americans with incomes of under $15,000, 12.7% have computers in their homes. The percentages climb steadily with income such that families who earn more than $75,000 annually have a 77.7% likelihood of owning a computer. The racial variable is often confounded with income, because Blacks and Hispanics make up a larger proportion of the lower income groups than do Whites.

Nonetheless, some racial differences continue to exist, even when income is statistically removed from the phenomenon. For example, the lowest likelihood of computer ownership is for Black households whose income is below $15,000 (7.7%). For all families earning less than $35,000, the percentage of White households owning computers is three times greater than the per centage of Black families and four times greater than the per centage of Hispanic families.

It is not only crucial that everyone has the access and knowledge to use computers and the Internet for the jobs for which they will compete upon finishing school, but it is also critical for school performance itself. Atwell and Battle examined survey data from a large number of eighth-grade students in the United States. They specifically noted the relationship between children's having access to a computer at home and their scores on standardized tests. They found that reading and math scores were related to home ownership of computers.

Not surprisingly, they also found that White students were more advantaged than Black students; wealthier students were more advantaged than poorer students. More surprisingly, the data showed that, controlling for the number of households who had computers, wealthy students obtained more of an advantage from their computer ownership than did poorer students, and White students obtained more of an advantage than Black students.

THE DIGITAL DIVIDE: THE SPECIAL CASE OF GENDER

Policymakers have good reason to worry about the digital divide. Wealth and socioeconomic status have frequently made education and employment opportunities more accessible to some than to others. Unequal distribution of wealth, even in the public sector, has created schools that are unequal in facilities, staff, and, in the end, academic performance of its students. The unbalanced relationship between race and socioeconomic status bears prime responsibility for the lower academic performance of traditionally underrepresented minorities. The cycle perpetuates itself as under-represented minorities are in a disadvantaged position to compete for the higher paying technology jobs of today's and tomorrow's workplace.

The same precipitating factors are more difficult to glean in the case of gender. Nonetheless, compared with men, women are underrepresented in their use and ownership of computers. Women take fewer technology classes in high school and college, are far less likely to graduate college with degrees in IT fields, are less likely to enroll in postgraduate technology fields, and are underrepresented in the higher end of technology jobs. A recent study by the American Association of University Women, for example, highlights how the vast majority of girls and women are being left out of the technology revolution.

The AAUW report shows that women and men are using computers as a "tool"- for accessing the Internet, using e-mail, and using word processing programs - at equal rates. However, there is a striking disparity in the number of women and men who are participating in the technological revolution at a more sophisticated level, the level that will allow them to be equal and active participants in the computer revolution that is taking classrooms and workplaces across the world by storm.

Women are conspicuously underrepresented in basic computer science education courses from a young age, and their lack of representation becomes more pronounced as they move through school. In 2001, women made up over 50% of all high school students, but only 17% of the students taking the Advanced Placement Computer Science A test in high school. The percentage of women fell to 11% for the more sophisticated Advanced Placement Computer Science AB test.

Only 4% of female college freshmen indicate that they intend to major in computer science. The gender disparity continues through college and on through computer science study at the graduate level. In 1999, despite their equal representation in college overall, women made up only 31% of the students majoring in computer science in the United States, and received only 16% of the computer science PhDs awarded in 1994.

As a direct consequence of the lack of formal computer education and training at the elementary, high school, and collegiate level, women make up only one out of five information technology professionals. According to many analysts, the number of women entering information technology professions is continuing to decline. The absence of girls and women from computer science classrooms prevents them from participating fully in the "new economy" later on in life and precludes them from earning the high salaries that sophisticated computer skills call forth in today's world. The fact that even more traditional fields of study are using computers to teach children basic materials leads to the possibility that computer assisted education - what the majority of educators believe is the future of education as we know it-has the potential for creating inequity in classroom education

Because the computer revolution is of recent origin, these examples of inequity brought about by computers reflect a relatively new problem. However, it is already the case that educators and researchers face a dilemma of gender inequity in the classroom. The Scholastic Aptitude Test (SAT), one of the most widely used instruments to assess college applicants, already shows reliable and pervasive differences between males and females, particularly in mathematics. This has received both scholarly and political recognition. We think it is clear that the dilemma of gender differences may well be exacerbated by reliance on the computer and the lack of attention paid to the differences in learning styles, motivations, and interests between boys and girls.

Although statistics clearly show pervasive gender inequity in the current computing situation, research has also shown that girls are as competent as boys when computing under certain conditions. As research psychologists, we find this situation an interesting one, because it suggests that there are factors beyond those of innate ability that are playing a large role in the current gender disparities.

TOWARD SOLUTIONS

Parents have provided boys and girls with their early views of themselves - their strengths, their weaknesses - as well as having shaped their views of what activities are appropriate to engage in. Parents not only communicate their own values and aspirations as they raise their children, but they also communicate the values of society at large. Children also learn from each other. Especially when they enter school, peers help to communicate society's attitudes to each other. If those attitudes include a view that computers are the province of boys, then peers can and do persistently reinforce those notions.

The formal educational system reinforces society's attitudes as well. Teachers, as particularly influential adults, may unwittingly communicate society's values about girls' ability in science, math, and technology to their students. Moreover, the very structure of classroom activities can multiply the problem by placing computer use in contexts that are public and competitive. The educational system chooses the software that will guide children's journey into the realm of technology. The frequent choice of male-oriented, competitive software continues to foster the digital divide.

In this chapter, we return to our discussion of developmental, contextual, and psychological factors to offer suggestions for overcoming the digital divide. Some suggestions are apparent; others are more subtle. Some require a great deal of effort and funding, but others require only awareness and the desire for change. We think that the primary impediment for change is the lack of awareness of the problem and the ways in which we all contribute to it. Armed with greater awareness, wise decision making by parents and educators can address the causes of computer anxiety, disidentification with computers, negative expectations, and inappropriate attributions at their roots. This chapter is dedicated to that goal.

UNDERSTANDING THE DIGITAL DIVIDE

Although we think that the model has much heuristic value as a road map organizing many of the important factors currently contributing to the digital divide, our intention here is not to provide an exhaustive list of all factors. We have represented important links between factors and concepts with arrows. In our model, we have focused our attention on the links that have been widely studied and are most relevant to our discussion. Additional research is needed to uncover other important linkages between some of the other concepts and to elaborate on the links that we have specified here.

At the heart of the digital divide is the individual student. She is the one experiencing computer anxiety, forming negative attitudes toward the computer, developing expectations for her performance, and, in certain contexts, performing more poorly on computer tasks. In the end, she is also the one who decides why she did not perform well on those tasks. The student must cope with her own level of computer anxiety, the attributions she makes about her level of ability and the degree of identification she experiences with computers. Anything that increases her computer anxiety, leads her to doubt her ability, or causes her to disidentify with computers will lead her to form negative attitudes about computers and technology.

Negative attitudes, in turn, will mean that she is more likely to avoid lessons, classes, and careers involving computers. Of course, anxiety, expectations, disidentification, and attributions are not independent and are related to each other in many ways. For instance, young women who do not identify with computers (i.e, feel that computers are not for people like them) may, in turn, feel more anxious when using computers. Young women who experience computer anxiety may also attribute any evidence of failure to their inability to understand technology. Nonetheless, it is useful to think of these processes operating within the individual as somewhat distinct, with each contributing to the digital divide in very direct ways.

As the model shows, the intra-individual variables are primarily affected by important influences in the social environment. We further divide the educational system into factors that are centered directly in the interpersonal contact between student and teacher and those that come from more structural elements of the school and classroom.

PARENTS

Parents are the primary socializing agents. From the first moments of life, parents represent the point of contact with the world. As children grow, parents select the toys, the books, and the entertainment to which the children are exposed. Children also learn much about themselves from the reactions of their parents. Are they cute? Are they smart? Do they like to read and write? The socialization goes on every day, much of it without deliberate thought. We begin by taking a look at some of the actions parents can take, even when their children are very young, to encourage girls to take their place in the technological revolution.

Learning what is appropriate for your gender. Children's concept of what it means to be a boy or a girl is rather fluid. Young girls believe that they can be boys if they dress like boys; young boys believe they can be girls if they dress like girls. The notion that gender is constant becomes clear to children near the age of 7. At this stage of development, children also learn to incorporate the social meaning of gender. They learn the attitudes and behaviours that accompany being a boy or girl. It is not too much of a caricature to say that boys learn that playing with trucks is in their domain. Playing with Barbie dolls is in the girls' domain.

Parents must be vigilant to disabuse children of unwanted gender stereotypes, especially near the age of gender constancy. Remember that stereotypes about what is appropriate for girls and boys can be quite subtle. They come from stories that we choose to read to our children, portrayals on television, and information provided by peers in school and in the backyard. Because parents are in an especially influential role, they can disabuse the stereotypes. They can make it clear to children that all types of choices are open to both boys and girls. Girls can and should do well at computers, mathematics, and science. If this message is instilled prior to the age of gender constancy, we will have a better chance to overcome the digital divide. Being attentive to the stereotype, the timing, and the remedy is a suggestion for all parents.

Encouraging positive attributions and expectations. Parents have been called the "expectancy socializers". As children grow and take on more tasks, parents form their own attitudes about their children's abilities. We saw that parents' attitudes and expectations about their children's performance affected the children's expectations as well. If parents believe that girls simply do not have the ability to tackle computer tasks, then the girls will take on the same attitude.

They will expect to fail. If girls do well at a task for which their parents believe they have limited ability, such as technology, then parents are likely to attribute the success to luck or to the possibility that it was merely an easy version of the task. If girls do not succeed at a computer task, parents attribute that failure to a lack of ability. More important, girls adopt the same set of attributions for themselves. Even a minor failure at a computer task, such as a momentary misunderstanding of the instructions, can lead girls to confirm their lack of ability. On the other hand, they credit luck for their success.

Once again, parental vigilance and awareness can ameliorate this problem. We must educate parents to understand that they, too, fall prey to the nefarious effects of society's stereotypes. All children need to be encouraged to see their successes at IT as testimony to their ability rather than to luck. It is certainly true that not all children can achieve unlimited heights on the computer, and it is important for children to have realistic assessments of their abilities.

It is even more important, though, not to limit children's quest for achievement just because the children are girls learning or working at a gender stereotypic task such as IT. Parents must convince themselves that girls have every bit the same ability at IT as boys and they must reinforce that attitude in their children. Make Computers Available to Daughters as Well as Sons; Encourage Their Use. Surveys show that parents are more likely to purchase computers for their sons than for their daughters. When they purchase computers, they spend more money on technology for boys than they do for girls. Girls report that they are less likely to have computers and they are less likely than boys to be encouraged to use them.

Parents must become as enthusiastic about encouraging their daughters to use computers as they are for their sons. We suspect that when girls use computers at home, parents think of it as cute. If they are not interested in computers, then so be it. However, when boys use computers at home, parents think of it as necessary. A lack of interest by boys in the family's PC or Mac is a disaster. It is necessary to remember that girls and boys have equal need to be comfortable on the computer. Whether it is playing a game, researching material, writing e-mail or doing homework, girls need to be encouraged to spend time on the family's computer. If the family does not have a computer for economic reasons, many schools and libraries have loaner programs or at least make computers available at their facilities.

Whenever possible, it is also important for boys and girls to see that adult women use the computer as well as adult men. Simply put, moms should spend time on the computer so that sons and daughters view technology as something that adults make use of rather than just dads. This will help boys and girls resist the idea that technology is gender linked - that is, that it is a toy or tool primarily for men. Another value of encouraging computer use at home is that it can provide a non-threatening context for teaching girls that making errors on the computer is acceptable.

Teachers have noted that girls seem afraid that they will break the machine if they hit the wrong key; boys seem to have no such worries. Indeed, in Robinson-Stavely and Cooper's (1990) studywith college students, women were far less likely to just try something when they needed to solve a problem. Men, on the other hand, made numerous attempts to find the solutions by simply trying many actions. Even though the majority of their attempts led nowhere, the mere willingness to try various solutions eventually produced success.

Parents and teachers can encourage girls not to fear making mistakes on the computer. Such lessons maybe more successful at home because of the less threatening environment that the home usually provides. Showing girls that the computer will not break because they tried incorrect key strokes, and that they have a greater chance to succeed at their task, will be a major help to girls as they proceed through school and into adulthood.

Consider Forming Voluntary Girls-Only Clubs. What kinds of experiences can make girls feel comfortable with technology? Voluntary after-school programs and summer camps can provide wonderful experiences to enhance children's comfort with computers. However, these well-intentioned activities may have the ironic consequence of undermining girls' confidence while enhancing only the boys'. We have seen that girls "vote with their feet," showing how they feel about technology by staying away in droves from voluntary mixed-gender computer activities.

The girls who do attend have to be strong enough to overcome several built-in traps that can make their experience less than positive. Not only may girls suffer from many of the social forces that tilt the playing field against them in the regular classroom, but in clubs and camps, the problem may be still worse. For example, anxiety due to the social context of computing, the nature of the software, and the effects of social stereotypes do not disappear merely because girls are participating with technology in extracurricular situations.

And, because camps and clubs have very few females who attend, it is likely that the girls who sign up for such activities will feel even more like token representatives of their gender, thus increasing their marginalization and stigmatization. It may also exacerbate the tendency for instructors to rely on male-oriented software and male-oriented examples. After all, the boys will so heavily outnumber the girls, that it may seem all the more natural to select material that intrigues boys rather than interests the few girls in the group.

Parents should seriously consider forming, or having their daughters join, computer clubs designed for exclusively for girls. Lichtman (1998) described a very successful girls-only computer club in Allentown, Pennsylvania. The Cyber Sisters Club opened its doors to 15 fifth-grade girls in the spring of 1998. Activities were based on the premise that girls will buy into technology primarily when they see how it relates to their own interests and preferences. Cyber Sisters focused on social activities such as chat rooms and e-mail.

It taught girls to find information on the Internet for special topics of interest, such as learning about the Backstreet Boys, the Spice Girls, Leonardo DiCaprio, and all-time favorites like Winnie the Pooh. Girls also learned how to create their own personal web pages and they "shopped" for graphics designs to beautify them. The 15 girls from Allentown, who had had only limited experience with computers prior to attending the Cyber Sisters Club, became highly enthusiastic and accomplished at using the computer.

Lichtman cites the nonthreatening atmosphere that was facilitated by not having to compete with boys and by teachers' attitudes that were pointedly encouraging and enthusiastic. In addition, the ability to use their time to focus on activities and examples that were consistent with girls' interests made the experience a relevant and rewarding one for girls. As we said earlier, computers in typical classrooms often function like communications designed for boys. In the Cyber Sisters Club, the communication was very directly related to girls, and they responded with enjoyment and enthusiasm.

Smith College, one of the premier women's colleges in the United States, offers a summer program exclusively for girls.

Its official Web site sets its mission in the following terms: "Girls can grow up to be great scientists. Many have. And yet, nearly a century after Marie Curie became the first person to win two Nobel Prizes, bright, ambitious high-school girls are often skeptical of their scientific abilities. " One of its 2001 campers commented at the end of the summer, "I've learned that being a girl and loving science is totally ok."

Parents should advocate for the creation of girls-only computer clubs and summer camps. We consider seriously the benefits and drawbacks of girls-only classes for technology and girls-only schools. In this section, however, we suggest that voluntary participation in clubs that are designed exclusively for girls can have productive and measurable benefits for girls. Schools will probably be cooperative with helping to create such experiences if parents request them.

So, too, will other civic groups, such as local YMCA/YWCA or community organizations. Giving girls the opportunity to learn in a way that makes them comfortable will allow them to see the benefits of technology for pursuing their own interests and exploring their own values. Once armed with sufficient skill, competence, and confidence, girls will be in a far better position to participate as equals in the computer experiences provided in their regular local schools. They may also gain the confidence and skill to participate more fully in the technological revolution that will characterize the rewarding careers of the 21st century.

THE CLASSROOM TEACHER

What can teachers do to help overcome the digital divide? Teachers are typically the first major influence on youngsters after the family itself. Whether it is pre-school, nursery school, or kindergarten, teachers become the first consistent representative of the social world beyond home. Their influence on the development of the child is enormous.

Teachers will play an essential role in any program designed to dispel the digital divide. Teachers can help to rectify mistaken ideas that children bring with them to school that may have been communicated by parents and peers. Teachers can carefully structure their classrooms in ways that minimize the negative effects of peers on girls' identification with computers.

Teachers can also monitor their own behaviour so that they neither cause nor exacerbate the reluctance that girls have about technology. Any adverse influence that a teacher may have on girls' conceptions of their ability and interest in pursuing computers and information technology is surely unintentional. Becoming aware of how they may be contributing to the digital divide and steps they may take to alleviate the problem will help teachers contribute to the solution.

Choose the Software Wisely. School systems pour an enormous amount of money into their technology programs. Much of the funding and the attention is devoted to hardware and operating systems. Should they purchase a mainframe? Should they purchase Macintosh or DOS system machines? Should they support UNIX? How shall they connect to the Internet? Shall there be computer classrooms, or shall every classroom have computers? Far less attention is spent on software. What tasks will children actually perform on the computer? What manufacturers produce good software programs? Will children actually learn something from those programs?

If they don't learn much, will they at least enjoy it? In many schools, teachers and principals are on their own when it comes to the daunting task of finding appropriate material to put on the computer. Many of the computer programs designed for young children contain the formal features that appeal to boys: competitive activities and story lines containing sports, space, or war. Girls are invited to learn from this software, but they certainly do not feel welcome.

Teachers must be especially vigilant to avoid any IT programs that rely on the factors that only boys prefer. Exploding missiles, the hitting of homeruns, and scoring of touchdowns may look appealing. They may come with sounds and lights that make us assume that they are motivating for children. As we have seen, however, these programs motivate boys, not girls. Avoiding such software is not an easy task for two reasons. One is that such software is prevalent in the educational market.

A second reason is that, unless we are extremely vigilant, we have a tendency to assume that computer software is appropriate when it is male-oriented. Recall the study by Huff and Cooper (1987). In that research, teachers eagerly wrote computer programs that were replete with male metaphors when they imagined that they were writing for students in general. Our automatic assumption that computers communicate with boys makes us vulnerable to missing the inappropriateness of the IT software for teaching girls.

What should appropriate software look like? This is not an easy question to answer, but we would like to raise an important issue. One suggestion is to create software that girls would enjoy, using some of the stories and characters that girls find appealing, and to have such software available in classrooms at all levels. Indeed, a mathematics program for girls might feature a digitized Barbie who needs to figure out the correct dimensions for making a dress. This would immerse Barbie and the student into solving geometric and algebraic problems.

Boys, on the other hand, could learn similar skills from an adventure in which their space ship traverses the planets of outer space. However, with this solution, we risk solving one problem by exacerbating another one. One value that marks modern education is an effort to eradicate inappropriate and unnecessary gender distinctions. Encouraging girls to identify with a gender-stereotypic character and permitting boys to continue to identify with aggressive adventures may permit both genders to perform well with computers. However, it will also reify the general social stereotypes about what is appropriate for girls and boys.

A second solution, and one that we endorse, is to search for gender-neutral software. Gender-neutral software would de-emphasize gender stereotypes of both kinds. Learning would not take place as a way to solve an intergalactic fight nor would it help Barbie create the latest fashion. Instead, it would be based on activities that are interesting to both sexes and are relevant to the educational task at hand. There are several good examples of such programs that have been successful in classrooms in recent years. We recommend that teachers be especially vigilant to find educationally appropriate, gender-neutral software for all phases of their classroom activities.

Provide Equal Access to Computers. Computers should be equally available to all students in a classroom. We doubt that teachers would ever intentionally create a situation in which boys have preferential access to computers. Nonetheless, in the real world of the classroom, it may often turn out that way. In the younger grades, computers are often available as optional activities. Teachers have commented that boys are the ones who more often choose to play their favorite games on the computer. Girls choose an alternate activity, or watch the boys play their computer games.

Although this is technically equal access, in reality it is not. Boys gravitate to the computers either because the software appeals to them or because of attitudes toward computers they have learned at home. Girls are not enamored by the software and may have entered school with more negative attitudes, possibly based on the stereotypes they learned at home. Choosing not to play with the computer when it is available adds to girls' self-conception that computers are not for them. We recommend that computers be used equally by all children. Every child, boy and girl, should have time scheduled for working with IT programs on the computer either in regular classrooms or in specially designated computer classrooms.

Attend to Boys and Girls ... Equally. Imagine Jared and Martha in their elementary school class. Each of them is attempting to learn how to master an exercise on the computer. When they have questions, will the teacher respond to Jared and Martha in the same way? Will the teacher call on each of them equally often? How will their work be evaluated? Most teachers believe that they treat boys and girls equally in their classrooms. Yet, research has shown that teachers unwittingly but systematically treat boys and girls differently.

In A Guide to Gender Fair Education in Science and Mathematics, Burger and Sandy (1998) report a few disturbing observations. When teaching science and math, teachers inadvertently initiate more interactions with boys than with girls; they call on boys more frequently than they call on girls, praise boys for the content of their work but praise girls for the appearance of their work.

Teachers respond differently to boys' and girls' requests for help. They are more apt to encourage boys to obtain answers for themselves while they tend to give girls the answers directly. In general, boys demand and receive more attention than girls. It is not surprising that girls emerge from such treatment with a lowered sense of efficacy, and less confidence in their ability to solve problems in information technology.

Burger and Sandy (1998) suggest that teachers carefully monitor their own behaviour to make certain that they are treating girls with behaviours that imply the same respect for their abilities and accomplishments that they convey to boys. They suggest that teachers ask themselves very systematic questions about their expectations and actions. Several checklists have been developed to help teachers monitor their own behaviour as they deliver instruction in technology, science, and mathematics.

Because gender bias in the classroom is almost always inadvertent, using self-rating scales and examining the objective observations of others can help teachers respond with equal encouragement, enthusiasm, and expectations to the boys and girls in their classrooms.

Reducing the problem of stereotype threat. Girls understand the stereotype that affects them: Computers are the province of boys, not girls. Girls are not supposed to enjoy working or playing with computers; they traditionally do less well at technology than boys. The forces acting on children, ranging from the attitudes of parents to the expectations of software manufacturers, have contributed to this belief. The problem with stereotypes is that they are often inaccurate and certainly do not apply to all members of the group. Yet, everyone knows their content. Members of the group that is negatively stereotyped feel the pressure, whether or not they endorse the stereotype and whether or not they believe the stereotype applies to them. We took a long look at research demonstrating the power of stereotype threat-studies that showed the effect of negative stereotypes on minority students' academic performance, female students' mathematics and technology achievements, and White students' accomplishments on athletic tasks.

As Steele (1997) has reminded us, stereotype threat is simply "in the air." It does not originate with any single source-not parents or teachers or peers-but rather stems from the general information structures that people have about their social world. Nonetheless, a growing body of research suggests that teachers may hold the key that can activate the antidote to this pernicious problem.

Wise Schooling: Providing feedback to overcome threat. In the movie Stand and Deliver, the teacher of a group of Latino students in an inner city high school in Los Angeles, California, challenged his class to take and pass the Advanced Placement exam in calculus. The teacher not only set his expectations very high, but also convinced his students that their mathematical knowledge was expandable beyond what they had allowed themselves to believe. His patient but challenging approach worked. His entire class received AP credit in calculus, an event so unlikely that it prompted the testing agency to question the results. What is most remarkable is that Stand and Deliver depicted the true story of teacher Jaime Escalante, who refused to allow his Latino students to succumb to the stereotype of inferior scholastic performance. He saw the potential in his students, challenged them to reach it, and convinced them of the truth that their ability would continue to grow as they worked, learned, and persisted.

By "wise schooling," Steele specifically refers to education that uses challenge and encouragement to find the essential humanity in people suffering under the threat posed by negative stereotypes. Challenge means that teachers establish high standards and expect their students to reach them. Encouragement is communicating to students that their intellectual ability is not immutable, but can grow with effort and practice. Jaime Escalante combined these variables and enabled his minority students to become proficient in mathematics. Can we adapt wise schooling policies to help women overcome the threat they experience in mathematics, science and technology? Can it help to overcome the digital divide?

Steele (1997) suggests several steps that schools and teachers can use to overcome stereotype threat that we heartily endorse in the context of women and computers. Suggestions include:

- Stress challenge over remediation. Girls in computer classes should be given challenging work that shows respect for their abilities and potential. Knowing that girls typically do not perform as well as boys at information technology tasks may prompt teachers to think remedially. Teachers may earnestly think that they should provide easier work so that the girls can "catch up." Wise schooling suggests this would be a mistake. People who feel threatened by a negative stereotype need to feel challenged to perform better.

- Stress the expandability of IT ability. Girls need to feel that their current performance is not the limit of what they can achieve. Dweck and her colleagues have shown that people differ in their tendency to think that intellectual performance is fixed versus mutable. Situational factors also play a role in this belief. Wise education stresses the mutability of intelligence and potential. If women students have spent years in classes feeling anxious about IT and worried about their level of ability, then knowing that their ability can grow with instruction and practice is crucial to overcoming the adverse effects.

- Value multiple perspectives. Wise education stresses that there is more than one way to be successful at IT tasks. Recall that, we introduced Turkle and Papert's (1990) observation that females think differently than males about how to approach the challenges in information technology. Wise education affirms the diversity of approaches to information technology.

- Make relevant role models available. Having women in the

roles of computer teacher and computer trouble-shooters offers "existence proofs" to students that negative stereotypes applied to women's capabilities at IT are not insurmountable.

Cohen *et al.* (1999) adapted two of the most important features of wise schooling in a particularly interesting experimental study. Although the content area of their study was not about technology, the research has clear implications for the digital divide. The investigators asked, "How can performance feedback be provided to people suffering from stereotype threat in a way that increases their motivation to do better? How can such feedback strengthen their identification with intellectual domains?" In their study, the stereotyped group was minority students at Stanford University, and the intellectual domain was the students' writing ability.

White and Black students participated in a study in which they were asked to write a letter of recommendation, nominating someone as their favorite teacher, mentor, or coach. They were led to believe that if their essay was sufficiently persuasive, it would be published in a professional journal. A week after writing their nominating essay, they returned to the laboratory and received feedback about their essay. The criticism, presumably written by a White university professor, contained hard-hitting but constructive criticisms ranging from sentence construction to overall impact of the essay. Students were encouraged to revise and resubmit their letters for possible publication.

In a third condition, students were provided with the challenge of the higher standard, asked for a resubmission, but not provided with the encouraging information. Other participants received the criticism without either the challenge or the encouragement. When students were then asked how motivated they were to pursue the writing task for possible publication, White students responded most positively to the challenge; the encouragement about their capabilities was unnecessary. Black students, however, who engage in academic tasks under the pressure of stereotype threat, responded most positively in the wise condition. The combination of challenge and encouragement made them more motivated to pursue publishing their article than any other type of feedback.

In the world outside of the laboratory, several universities have implemented novel programs to encourage higher performance by students in traditionally stigmatized groups based on the elements of wise schooling. The University of Michigan implemented such a program for minority and non-minority freshmen students. The program emphasizes that it is nonremedial, challenging, and expects high achievement of participants. The program provides enrichment challenges including additional voluntary seminars, extra outside speakers, and discussion groups. Students are encouraged to view their academic potential as expandable.

After a semester of participating in the program, minority and White students did very well in their coursework. The effect was most dramatic for minority students, however. Their grades were significantly higher than the grades of minority students who were not in the program, even controlling for previous ability as measured by standardized admissions tests. There is yet another result from the University of Michigan data that is relevant to the digital divide. In this book, we have seen that even women with excellent GPAs and other indicants of ability to grasp technology still feel anxious and uncomfortable.

They underperform at IT tasks and underenroll in IT courses, compared to what one would expect from their level of ability. The same phenomenon typifies the performance of Black students in college. Relative to the their high school GPAs and scores on standardized tests, Black students typically attain poorer grades in college courses than do White students with similar high school records and test scores. After participating in the wise schooling, the underperformance of Black students at the University of Michigan disappeared.

Every teacher in every classroom can apply the wise schooling approach. It requires awareness on the part of teachers and school systems that girls and women are constantly subjected to the pressure of stereotype threat in technology, science, and mathematics. Reducing standards and expectations will not contribute to a solution. Rather, the curriculum must be built upon challenges that raise rather then lower the bar for success, raise expectations for what girls are expected to accomplish, and provide encouragement based on the girls' growing capacity to master technology.

This is as true at the kindergarten level as it is at the university. Girls should be expected to work with computers with as much frequency and enthusiasm as boys do, whether it is learning letters from a computer program at age 5 or learning about the growth of dendrites at age 18. Moreover, guidance counselors and administrators need to provide similar wise challenges to girls and women who are choosing their academic courses. Is it all right that high school girls opt out of higher level computer courses? Wise schooling says no. The wise schooling of the future mandates that girls and women be challenged to improve their computer skills in the most demanding ways provided by the curriculum. With such challenge and encouragement, educators can take major steps to eliminate the gender-based, digital divide.

TEACHER TRAINING

We cannot emphasize too strongly the importance of teacher training. School systems spend considerable time and money to provide continuing education and training for teachers. Teacher training in the area of technology is particularly important. Few teachers received substantial education in computers during their own college education and, moreover, the advances in technology are so rapid that training needs to be continual.

Every upgrade in computer capability requires training. Every upgrade in the district's operating system requires training. In many school systems, the training in how to use the hardware is available. However, the digital divide is not a function of the operating system or the size of the computers' RAM. Teachers would welcome and would benefit from school systems providing help and support for overcoming the digital divide. Most teachers are unaware of the problem caused by the selection of software, the structure of the classroom, and the social context of the computing environment.

The concepts within the wise schooling approach can be taught, but teachers need to be given the opportunity to learn them. We encourage school districts to pay as much attention to the social aspects of computing as they do to the technology hardware. Teacher training is essential to promote awareness of the problem and the tools for overcoming it.

Classroom Structure

The structure of the classroom, from pre-school to college, is very much determined by the teacher. However, some facets of classroom life affect students' attitudes and behaviours so directly that even the most well-intentioned teacher who monitors his or her own behaviour carefully may still structure the classroom in a way that unwittingly contributes to the digital divide.

Attending to the Social Context

One of the more pervasive antecedents of girls' and women's computer anxiety is the social context in which computing is performed. Throughout this book, we have discussed research showing that girls' IT work and attitudes are markedly affected by the social composition of their learning groups. When girls work in mixed-gender, competitive groups, their computer attitudes become more negative, their anxiety is heightened, and their performance deteriorates.

Research has also shown that, in some circumstances, groups of any kind can be harmful to girls' interest in and ability at computing. Boys often profit from a public social context, but girls do not. This is especially true when the story lines of IT software are oriented toward boys, such as when computer programs use adventure story formats. This research leads us to suggest that classrooms providing private space for individuals to conduct their computing maybe beneficial to girls. Allocation of private space can be done in both regular classroom setting or in computer cluster environments. If individualized instruction is attempted, the computing space should be one in which no other students are present.

Although it may be expensive to provide private space, it is more costly to the social and economic capital to diminish the computational ability and interest of half of the population.

If the activities and resources make private computing impossible, another possible solution is to use same-sex computer learning groups, in which girls work together on computer problems.

Although we hesitate to suggest that computer education necessarily must be segregated by gender, same-sex education is currently a hotly debated issue in education, and we thoroughly examine the pros and cons of separate schooling and/or separate classrooms for girls and boys. To the degree that same-sex learning groups mitigate the anxiety and the competition that arises in mixed-sex groups, we think it is wise to offer girls the opportunity to do their computational learning with children of the same gender.

Fostering learning by cooperation: The Jigsaw Classroom. In addition to private computing and same-sex learning, there is an intriguing alternative approach that, used in conjunction with the suggestions on social context, may be able to reduce anxiety and overcome some of the other adverse consequences of public, mixed-gender contexts: Make both sexes integral to solving a problem through interdependent computer tasks. This approach holds promise as a way to both mitigate computer anxiety and lead girls and young women to feel a sense of identification with and ownership of technology. Mixed-sex groups in computer contexts present three major problems, all of which are related to boys' greater experience with computers: computer anxiety, gender-based exclusion, and too much helping. If classes are planned to circumvent these problems, then boys and girls may be able to work together in a way that will benefit both sexes.

Studies of cooperative learning techniques show that cooperative strategies can be effective not only in facilitating learning, but also in increasing feelings of inclusion and cooperation among diverse groups of students. More than 60 studies, many conducted by research centers sponsored by the federal government or by local school districts, show that when teachers structure their classroom assignments such that all students are integral to solving common problems (interdependent goals) and each student has individual accountability, students' achievement goes up. Since they focus students on teamwork and cooperation, rather than competition, cooperative learning environments also provide a more comfortable working environment, one that will likely reduce computer anxiety.

A widely used cooperative strategy that is particularly useful in the context of teaching technology is the Jigsaw Classroom. Designed by Elliot Aronson and his graduate students at the University of Texas, Jigsaw classes are constructed so that the individual students must rely on each other when completing classroom assignments. In contrast to the more traditional competitive learning environments, the interdependent focus of the Jigsaw strategy ensures that all students in a classroom participate equally in learning as they work together as a cooperative group to complete classroom assignments.

In Jigsaw classrooms, students are assigned to small groups of about four members, and each group should be mixed with regard to race, gender and ability. Each group of students is then given an assignment that has been divided into four unique and non-overlapping parts. Individual group members take one of the parts as their personal assignment. This way, each student is responsible for one piece of his or her group's assignment, and each piece has equal importance in the completion of the group assignment.

Once students are assigned their individual parts, they become their group's "expert" on that topic, and are allowed to consult with other "experts" who have been assigned the same piece in the other groups. For instance, if the group project was to design a web page, one student may be in charge of figuring out how to import photographs to the page, another may be in charge of writing the text of the page, another may be in charge of learning to insert a button to collect data from web visitors, and another may be assigned the task of learning how to change the font and style of the page.

After students have completed their portion of the assignment, they return to their original group to present their work. At that time, the members within each group must work together to integrate each member's individual piece into the final group assignment. To return to our web page design scenario, once the students convene as a group, they must assemble the different pieces they have learned into a larger whole, the page itself. Because each individual group member is the only one in the group who has knowledge about his or her individual piece, he or she must teach it to the other group members.

The interdependence among students fosters collaboration rather than competition among the group members. It is in each group's best interest if all of its members succeed. Excluding members is not beneficial because each group member suffers if one of their peers does not do well on his or her part.

An important aspect of Jigsaw learning is that students are tested on all of the aspects of the topic area. For this reason, they must rely on the other members of their group when completing the assignment or learning the material. Grading may be done on the group level, as in a group project grade, or the individual level, as in an individual quiz, but students must learn the information for each piece of the project.

Overall, tests of the Jigsaw method and other cooperative learning techniques have shown positive results. Jigsaw methods promote discussion among the group members and foster participation and contribution from all students. After working in interdependent groups, students report greater liking for school and also report higher levels of self-esteem. Students also report better relationships with their peers, shown by increased liking for their classmates.

Importantly, the increased liking among classmates appears to reduce intergroup conflict, as students' increased liking spans gender and racial boundaries. Also, the increased feelings of acceptance and inclusion in Jigsaw classes' leads previously poorly perform students to show more improvement than they do in more traditional classes. We believe that girls and young women may receive similar benefits if Jigsaw methods are used in computer classes. If girls and young women feel included in computer learning rather than left with the feeling that the course is really not for people like them, they will be more likely to identify with the topic, enjoy the course more and show superior performance.

One reason why Jigsaw learning may work especially well with computer lessons is the widely varying skills students bring to computer classrooms. Some students may enter the classroom more familiar with programming tasks than others. Instead of being bored while waiting for the other students to catch up, Jigsaw classes provide a structure in which advanced students can essentially become "teachers" and help their peers with less sophisticated skills.

As girls and boys learn from each other in their expert groups, they can utilize the knowledge of their fellow students as a resource for more basic questions. The classroom teacher is then freed to spend time answering more sophisticated questions, and to monitor the group learning situation to make sure that no student is having difficulty completing the basics of his or her assignment. The fact that each student is ultimately responsible for relaying her or his knowledge back to their group, ensures that each student learn the material well enough to "teach" it to their peers.

Cooperative learning techniques such as the Jigsaw method may also go a long way toward alleviating computer anxiety. Because the students have their expert groups to consult with and fall back on, cooperative learning may help dispel the anxiety that often accompanies computer use. Instead of being forced to compete for the attention of a busy teacher or to compete with other students to see who can finish the fastest, students are encouraged to use their fellow students as a resource, thus potentially alleviating their arousal and anxiety.

Overall, the research strongly suggests that the Jigsaw method and other cooperative learning techniques do admirably well in increasing student performance and providing a comfortable classroom environment. We think that such learning strategies will be productive in helping young women identify with computers and overcome the anxiety that some feel when performing computer tasks.

We believe that adoption of the suggestions outlined in this chapter can go a long way toward increasing girls' and young women's identification with computers and making them feel more comfortable when using IT. Parents and teachers alike must be vigilant in assessing the way that their interactions may affect girls' and young women's attitudes toward computers. Challenging girls to develop positive expectations for themselves at crucial ages, providing them with the opportunities for learning about computers in environments that lessen anxiety and paying attention to the factors that lead to disidentification will be crucial factors in giving girls a vision of how IT may benefit them in the future.

SINGLE-SEX

Of all the solutions proposed to remedy the gender gap in science and technology, none has generated more controversy than the fierce and often emotional debate over single-sex education. And all signs suggest that the controversy will continue to rage on in the months and years to come. The U. S. Department of Education recently announced a plan to amend the Title IX section of the Education Amendment of 1972. Title IX is the section that prohibits federally funded programs from excluding students because of their gender. It ensures, for instance, that girls and boys in public schools have equal access to athletic programs.

And to this point, most have viewed it as prohibiting federally funded single-sex schools. The new changes, supported by Senators Hillary Rodham Clinton, Kay Bailey Hutchison, and other key female and male politicians, center around single-sex education. In its own words, the purpose of the amendment is "... to provide more flexibility for educators to establish single-sex classes and schools at the elementary and secondary levels."

In the past several decades in the United States, experimentation with single-sex education has been largely confined to private school environments. Of the 89,508 operating public elementary and secondary schools in the country, only 11 are currently single sex. Some attribute public schools' reluctance to experiment with single-sex education to administrators' fear of sex discrimination lawsuits based on Title IX. The new amendment will likely open the floodgates and ensure that single-sex options are more widely available in public school settings. In fact, the new amendment, if passed, may dramatically change the structure of public school classrooms as we know them.

Is single-sex schooling really the solution to remedying the science and technology gender gap? Some parents seem to think so. A glance at the statistics surrounding single-sex schools at the elementary and secondary levels indicates a renewed interest in single-sex education. Applications to single-sex schools increased 40% from the period 1991 to 2000, and 31 new single-sex schools opened in the country between 1997 and 2002. At the same time that many have showed a renewed interest in single-sex education, a number of organizations, among them the American Association of University Women (AAUW), have spoken out in favour of co-education.

The popular media has been following the debate by reporting on case studies, research, and the philosophical positions held by notable public figures as well as parents and teachers directly involved in the schools. The reports reflect the wide range of opinions that exists both in the academic community and in the public sphere.

Many reports espouse what appear to be remarkable benefits of single-sex schooling. Consider the Young Women's Leadership School of East Harlem, for instance. The Young Women's Leadership School is a public all-girls secondary school located in East Harlem, New York. The experimental school was created in 1996; although it is public, it was helped along by a large financial contribution from philanthropist Ann Tisch.

The Young Women's Leadership School is the first single-sex public school to operate in New York since the 1970s, and its purpose is to provide young women from Harlem a chance to focus on their studies without the distraction of boys. So far, the school has been a great success. Most students at the Young Women's Leadership School are from demographic groups that usually underperform academically. For instance, the large majority of students come from economically disadvantaged backgrounds; almost 75% of the class of 2001 came from families classified as below the poverty line. The school also reflects Harlem's racial composition-over 95% of the students are Black or Latina.

Students at this school have beaten the socio-structural odds. Students at the Young Women's Leadership School dramatically outperform their peers at co-educational public schools. Last year, 100% of the students at the Young Women's Leadership School passed the English part of the New York Regents exam, in comparison to only 42% of New York City students overall.

All but one of the young women in the class of 2001 was accepted to a 4-year college, even though a full 90% were the first member of their family to attend college. There is no question that the experience was a dramatic success for the students. Still, some have questioned whether the single-sex environment is responsible for the students' academic suecess or instead, whether the academic performance differences are attributable to the financial support, good teachers, and small classes provided by the school.

Other highly publicized experiments in single-sex education also appear successful, at least anecdotally. The Seattle Girls' School (SGS), all-girls middle school focused on math and science education, is another school that has received recent media attention. The Seattle Girls School (SGS) is an example of single-sex experimentation in the private sphere. Started in 2001 with a $500,000 seed grant from the Bill and Melinda Gates Foundation, the school's mission is to encourage young women to participate in the sciences.

Teachers, parents, and students affiliated with the school report that the all-girls environment allows young women to focus on academics without the distraction of boys. They feel that the all-girls environment empowers young women to pursue and succeed at careers in traditionally male-dominated fields such as mathematics and science. And the list goes on.

The students at Western High, an all-girls public school in Baltimore, like students at the Young Women's Leadership School, come from economically and racially diverse backgrounds; more than one third met the school district's qualifications for subsidized lunches.

Regardless, the young women at this school consistently outperform other students in their school district on a battery of important academic outcome variables. In 2001, their average SAT scores were more than 100 points higher than the district-wide average. Western High students also took more Advanced Placement examinations than did students at any of the other schools in their district, and over 90% of the class of 2001 attended college directly after high school graduation.

Despite these highly publicized positive outcomes, not everyone agrees that single-sex schools are the best option for students. Perhaps the most vivid evidence of controversy occurred soon after the Young Women's Leadership School of East Harlem opened its doors to their first class of young women. Almost immediately, both the New York chapter of the American Civil Liberties Union (ACLU) and the National Organization of Women (NOW) filed lawsuits against the school, arguing that it should be closed immediately because it violated the "equal access" clause of Title IX.

Although to date the Young Women's Leadership School is still open, similar lawsuits forced the Malcolm X Academy to go co-educational. Are the positions of NOW and ACLU the bastions of civil rights and equal opportunity, or are they striking a blow against the most radical and effective attempts to break down the racial and gender barriers? Apart from the prescriptions and proscriptions of Title IX and other Constitutional issues, we need to address the question of what is gained and what is lost from an educational perspective if children are taught in single-sex environments.

Some believe that single-sex education maybe used as a "band aid" approach to remedy problems in our education system that should demand longer term solutions-problems such as securing better training for teachers in all school districts, instituting smaller class sizes, spending money on better facilities, and working to improve student discipline. Co-education advocates note that many of the successful single-sex programs differ from the standard schools not only in their sex composition, but also in their smaller teacher-student ratios overall, smaller classes, and superior facilities.

They attribute the incredible success of students to these structural factors rather than gender separation per se. Others decry the fact that single-sex schools encourage segregation. They wonder why educators in the first decade of the 21st century would start revisiting the idea of sex segregation 30 years after Equal Rights Amendment supporters struggled to make all public school facilities equally accessible to both boys and girls.

Others believe that co-educational settings may help young men and women prepare for the future by providing important social benefits. That is, students in co-educational elementary and secondary schools may become better prepared for a mixed-sex professional and family life. This position was elaborated in an Atlantic Monthly article questioning the benefits of single-sex schooling. Still others argue that rather than dispelling gender stereotypes, single-sex schools may end up encouraging them.

In this chapter, we analyze the benefits and drawbacks of single-sex education as a solution to the gender equity problem in science and technology. Single-sex education is both an extremely important issue and a very complicated one. It is also a timely issue. With the revisions to Title IX, federal, state, and local governments will soon face important decisions about how to structure not only classes, but also schools themselves.

As parents and educators, we must be cognizant of the issues so that we can make the best decisions for the students of today and tomorrow. Our intention is not to solve this important question in this chapter, but rather to inform the debate. There are important lessons to be learned from the research and from the ideas that are currently being debated. We know that a greater understanding and knowledge of the issues can give us insight into how to provide young women with more opportunities to learn about and benefit from computers, technology, and science.

THE SINGLE-SEX/CO-EDUCATION DEBATE

Educators, scholars, parents, and students argue for the co-educational status quo for any of a number of philosophical and political reasons. Some co-education advocates question whether single-sex education benefits students academically at all. Rather, they think that the studies showing superior education benefits for single-sex schools and classrooms are flawed in important ways. Others acknowledge that there may be some educational benefits, but think that they are outweighed by the social drawbacks of single-sex settings.

Still other co-education proponents advocate the status quo for philosophical reasons. They argue that sex-segregated schooling is regressive. Important gains have been made in the past 40 years in gender equality in education. For instance, the last strongholds of sex segregation, like the Virginia Military Institute, have been eradicated. In their opinion, the drawbacks of sex segregation, like racial segregation, outweigh the potential educational benefits that may be realized in single-sex settings. A deeper analysis of the positions both in favour and against single-sex schooling shows some important facts, and we discuss the two positions in more detail in the next section.

Proponents of single-sex schools argue that putting boys and girls together in the classroom is detrimental for students, and particularly detrimental for girls. One reason for this claim is based on the activation of stereotypes when gender is a focal issue. Having boys and girls together in the same school keeps the cognitive representation of gender in the forefront. In a co-educational environment, boys' facility and experience with technology and their skill at math and science encourages positive attitudes and higher performance. For girls, co-education in technology, math, and science brings anxiety, negative attitudes, and inhibited performance.

Activating the gender concept makes it more probable that teachers will inadvertently select male-oriented software and examples for their computer classrooms. Moreover, highlighting gender will allow that "threat in the air" to place its heavy burden on the girls in the school, whether they believe the social stereotype or not. The increased spotlight on gender may also draw attention to sex roles and sex stereotypes. This may encourage both females and males to pursue more sex-stereotyped courses of study, either because they think of themselves in more gendered terms, or in order to fit in with their peers. If females and males choose areas of study based on gender stereotyped roles, this will contribute to the gender disparities seen in the higher education and employment sector.

Social Concerns

A second class of reasons that supports single-sex education stems from the social concerns of both boys and girls. Proponents points out those students have only limited time and attention that they can allocate to either academic or social concerns. Co-educational settings presumably shift students' attention away from the academic sphere to the social sphere. Boys and girls, particularly in the middle and high school years, may be distracted from their studies by concerns about their popularity, appearance, and relationships.

Co-education has to fight through the social relationships to convince students to focus on their education rather than each other. Proponents of this argument conclude that single-sex education will be equally beneficial for boys and for girls, relative to the typical co-educational alternative.

Teacher Attention

Other arguments favoring single-sex education draw directly from classroom observation research. Boys in mixed-sex classrooms receive more classroom resources than girls. Without being aware of it, teachers give boys more attention and more constructive encouragement than they give girls in the same classrooms. As a result, girls learn less course material and feel less confident about their academic performance than boys. Advocates of single-sex education claim that separating the sexes will minimize these factors. If so, single-sex settings at crucial times in students' academic self-concept development may help to remedy the current gender inequalities in science and computer attitudes and achievement.

Student Interaction Patterns

Interaction patterns of the students themselves may also create an uneven playing field for girls. Although males and females appear to have similar personality types, sex differences nonetheless arise when children interact in mixed-sex contexts. And these sex differences appear to benefit boys. Jacklin and Maccoby (1978), for instance, had girls interact with other students in pairs. The girls were paired either with a boy or with another girl. The researchers then timed how long each child sat back and looked on as their partner played with the toys. When the girls were paired with other girls, they rarely sat by and watched as the other played. Thus, the researchers concluded that girls are not less assertive or inactive by nature. However, girls in mixed-sex pairs tended to defer to their male partners. These girls spent a significant amount of time sitting by and watching as their male partners took over control of the toys.

Other studies have corroborated the findings that when boys and girls interact in mixed-sex settings, boys tend to dominate the available resources. Powlishta, for instance, studied what happened when mixed-sex pairs were left alone in a playroom with an attractive toy. When the pairs were left unsupervised, boys ended up spending more time with the toy than the girls. Gender differences in interaction styles may be the reason why boys tend to take over resources in mixed-sex settings.

Girls interacting in cooperative activities tend to use polite suggestions to get their opinions and desires across. In contrast, boys of the same age tend to use direct commands to achieve their goals. Research shows that boys begin to ignore or discount girls' polite suggestions around the time that the children are about to enter school. The developmental psychologist Eleanor Maccoby (1990) concludes that many of the gender differences in interaction styles have their roots in the rules and norms that develop in children's playgroups when they are very young. Children spend much of their time in sex-segregated playgroups, and the playgroups for each gender develop different norms for interactions.

Boys in same-sex groups tend to use direct speaking styles, tend to interrupt each other more in conversation, and more often refuse to obey each others' orders than girls in same-sex groups. In contrast, interactions within all-girl groups tend to be focused more on relationships. Girls tend to be more polite in their interactions with each other, they tend to wait patiently for other group members to finish speaking before interrupting, and they tend to suggest rather than command. Some researchers have referred to the different norms that arise in different sex playgroups as distinct "cultures".

Boys and girls grow accustomed to their typical playgroup interaction styles. But the styles females have learned may put them at a disadvantage when members of the two "cultures" meet and engage in mixed-sex interaction. For this reason, girls interacting in mixed-sex settings may end up contributing less to group discussions in school. In mixed gender computer and mathematics classes, and girls and young women do not participate as actively as their male peers.

To the degree that "hands on" learning leads to more positive computer attitudes and performance, girls in mixed-sex settings will be disadvantaged. In light of the research on teacher attention and students' interaction patterns, some proponents of single-sex schools argue that although co-education looks like "equal access" on the outside, the classroom dynamics it engenders makes it not equal in reality. They believe that girls will benefit from, and become empowered in, environments where they are not competing with boys for classroom resources.

Role Models

Another argument in favour of single-sex schooling is that they tend to provide more same-sex role models in instructional roles in math, science, and computer classes than do mixed-sex environments. Note that it is not necessary for the teachers in same-sex schools to be of the same gender as their pupils. Nonetheless, same-sex schools tend to have a higher proportion of instructors of the relevant gender. Some have argued that male teachers may be more likely than female ones to make stereotypic inferences about female students, and thus may end up dissuading female students either consciously or unconsciously from pursuing study in traditionally male-dominated topics.

Female teachers in topics such as math, science, and computers may also help to break down the sex-stereotypes that surround these topics of study. Research suggests that female role models have positive effects on female employees, and some have argued that female teachers in areas like math, science, and computers will lead to similar positive outcomes.It thus seems that there are five major reasons that girls, in particular, may benefit from single-sex schools:

1. Single-sex schools allow students to focus more exclusively on academics because they provide fewer social distractions.
2. Single-sex schools may lessen students' adoption of sex-stereotyped preferences.
3. Single-sex schools may alleviate problems of sex-skewed classroom resource allocation.
4. Single-sex schools may allow students to participate more equally at crucial points in their academic self-concept development.
5. Single-sex schools tend to provide more same-sex role models, which may help to break down sex stereotypes and alleviate problems of tokenism.

CO-EDUCATION PROPONENTS

On the other side of the fierce controversy are proponents of the co-education status quo. These educators and researchers argue that co-educational settings are superior to single-sex ones for a number of reasons, including:

1. Mixed-sex schools more accurately reflect the reality of the social world. Thus, they do the best job of preparing students for the future where they will inevitably face a mixed-sex workplace, family life, and social life.

2. Rather than dispelling gender stereotypes, sex segregation in schools may actually inadvertently reinforce them by drawing students' and teachers' attention to the idea that there are gender differences in interests and learning styles.
3. Segregating students by sex may put young women in victim roles. Perhaps students will infer that girls have their own class or school because they have inferior academic skills and ability.

VERSUS MIXED

Throughout this volume, we have relied heavily on empirical research to raise questions and suggest answers. In this section, we examine studies that have compared students attending single-sex versus co-educational schools on a number of important academic outcome variables. We will see whether type of school appears to influence students' attitudes toward math, science, and technology, their academic confidence in these areas, the degree to which they endorse gender stereotypes, and their academic performance. We will also look at whether type of school impacts students' plans for the future, such as their anticipated career choices.

The research comparing girls' and boys' outcomes as a function of school type is extensive, and the findings are not always completely consistent across studies. One reason for the inconsistencies is, in many cases, the single-sex schools studied differ from the co-educational control schools in important ways beyond the single-sex/co-educational variable of interest. For example, most single-sex schools in the United States are private, and vary in their selectivity in accepting applicants.

In order to test whether the sex composition of the school is responsible for any differences in student performance, confidence, or future professional choices, researchers must find co-educational control schools that are equally selective, and are also similar on other important variables such as family income, race, and so on. In addition to these methodological difficulties, there may be important demographic differences in the type of parents that send their children to single-sex versus mixed-sex schools. These sorts of pre-existing demographic differences can influence students' confidence, achievement, and plans for the future in systematic ways.

Most of the studies we review here pay as careful attention as possible to these issues and attempt to control for extraneous factors like pre-existing demographic differences between students in single-sex and co-educational schools in their analyses. However, the control procedures are not always perfect, which sometimes leave results open to interpretation. Despite the important methodological issues that arise when comparing self-selected groups, we believe that the research is informative and important and, when examined critically and taken as a whole, we think it can give us clues about how to increase young women's opportunities in science and technology.

Much of the research on single-sex schools was designed to analyze students' performance and attitudes about math and science. Although technology brings with it additional dimensions that are troubling to females, such as the sex-stereotyping of the IT software, most of the data about attitudes and performance in the male-stereotyped domains of math and science apply equally well to computer attitudes, confidence, and performance.

ATTITUDES, ACADEMIC SELF-ESTEEM, ACADEMIC CONFIDENCE

Do young women who attend single-sex schools feel more positively toward math, science, and technology than young women attending co-educational schools? Some reports suggest that single-sex environments do provide academic advantages to girls beyond those provided by co-educational environments. If single-sex schools lead young women to form more positive attitudes toward computers, math, and science and lead them to express increased confidence in their abilities in those traditionally sex-typed fields, this might be a first step in encouraging them to study these topics at the collegiate or graduate level.

Some studies show that young women attending all-girls secondary schools hold more positive attitudes toward traditionally male-dominated topics of study than young women of the same age attending co-educational schools. Gwizdala and Steinback (1990), for example, surveyed 722 young women attending either a single-sex or a co-educational college preparatory school.

Their study showed that students at the all-girls school held more positive attitudes toward mathematics in general and more positive attitudes toward their own ability in mathematics than students attending the co-educational comparison school. The all-girls school students also reported more comfort when asking questions in their math classes than co-educational school students. When asked how they would feel about learning in a mixed-sex setting, the young women at the all-girls school reported that they thought their performance would suffer in co-educational classes.

Other studies also show that young women attending all-girls schools have more positive attitudes toward math and the physical sciences than girls at co-educational schools. In fact, research looking at both boys' and girls' attitudes as a function of type of school show an interesting pattern.

Co-educational settings seem to lead students to hold attitudes that are in line with the gender stereotypes of the area of study. Young men in co-educational schools hold more positive attitudes toward, and feel more confident in, their abilities in traditionally male-dominated fields like math and physical science. In contrast, young women in co-educational settings tend to report more positive attitudes and confidence in traditionally female sex-typed areas like English and biology.

There is some indication that single-sex settings minimize the effects of these gender stereotypes. Young women in single-sex schools are more positive toward and more confident in traditionally male sex-typed areas of study compared to their female peers at co-educational schools. In contrast, young men are less favorable toward and confident in traditionally male sex-typed areas of study than are their male peers in co-educational schools.

Lawrie and Brown (1992) surveyed 284 British students aged

14-15 in order to assess how school type impacted their attitudes toward mathematics. Their study showed that single-sex environments were beneficial to girls, but that mixed-sex environments were slightly more beneficial to boys. Girls attending the all-girls school reported enjoying math significantly more than a control group of girls attending a co-educational school. Girls in the single-sex environment also reported that they found math less difficult than girls in co-educational schools, although this difference did not reach statistical significance. The pattern for boys was somewhat different.

Type of school did not impact boys' reported enjoyment of math. However, boys attending the all-boys school reported more difficulty with math than did boys attending the mixed school. The pattern of attitude scores indicates that girls' outcomes improve when boys are not in the school, but that boys may actually benefit from having girls in the school. One possibility is that boys receive advantages from being labeled a "male" in mixed-sex environments. Since the stereotypes benefit boys in math, they might think of themselves as having more ability when their sex is made salient by the presence of girls in the classroom. Boys in all-boys schools, however, receive no benefits from the positive male stereotypes because they apply to all the students in the school.

Lawrie and Brown also looked at whether school type was correlated with students' intentions to pursue study of various academic topics in the future. To test this, they asked students to indicate in which subjects they would take A-level examinations (competitive exams) if they remained in school for the following year. Results showed a similar pattern to the attitude items described already. Girls attending the all-girls schools were more than twice as likely to predict taking A-levels in math (14.7%) than were girls in the mixed school (6.7%).

Girls in the mixed school, on the other hand, were more likely to express interest in taking English A-levels (26%) than were girls in the single-sex school (16.3%). Results from the boys were the opposite. Boys at the all-boys schools indicated less interest in the physics A-levels (9%) than did boys attending the co-educational school (23%), but were more interested in the languages A-levels (17%), a traditionally female sex-typed area of study, than their same-sex counterparts attending mixed schools (6%).

Thus, the Lawrie and Brown (1992) study suggests that the gender composition of the school interacts with sex-typed areas of study. Boys and girls in mixed-sex settings tend to like topics that are sex typed for their gender. In contrast, single-sex settings appear to provide some respite from rigid gender stereotyping. Girls tend to like math and physical science more, and boys tend to like traditional female topics more, under single-sex conditions.

Harvey and Stables (1986) focused on the benefits of same-sex schooling for the physical sciences. They surveyed 2,300 students at single- and mixed-sex schools in southwest England about their attitudes toward various scientific disciplines. The pattern of results for science attitudes paralleled those found by Lawrie and Brown (1992) for math attitudes. Girls at all-girls schools were more positive toward science in general, and physics and chemistry in particular, than girls attending mixed-sex schools. Results for attitudes toward biology, a traditionally female discipline, showed an advantage in favour of mixed-sex settings.

Although boys' attitudes toward science in general or chemistry in particular did not differ by type of school, their attitudes toward physics paralleled those found by Lawrie and Brown (1992). Boys attending mixed-sex schools had more positive attitudes toward physics than boys in all boys' schools. In contrast, single-sex settings lessened the stereotyped behaviour. Boys attending all-boys schools had more positive attitudes toward the traditionally female discipline of biology than did boys in mixed-sex schools.

Other studies also offer support for the notion that young women attending all-girls schools have more positive attitudes toward math and science than same-sex peers attending co-educational schools. Colley *et al.* (1994) asked students to indicate preferences for areas of study. Results from students in the 11-12 age group showed that girls attending single-sex schools showed stronger preferences for math and science than same-aged peers attending co-educational schools. Boys attending single-sex schools showed stronger preferences for music and art than boys attending co-educational schools.

Another important outcome variable measured in the research is academic self-esteem or academic self-confidence. Research shows that young women's choices about future coursework choices and career choices are influenced by their confidence. Therefore, it is important to know whether type of school influences academic self-esteem and self-confidence. Cairns (1990) suggested that young women attending single-sex schools may be more academically self-confident than those attending mixed-sex schools.

He surveyed middle school students attending academically focused single-sex and mixed-sex schools in Ireland. Results from his study showed that young women attending the single-sex schools had higher levels of academic self-esteem and stronger internal loci of control than a group of same-aged peers who attended co-educational schools, even when the two groups were equated on their socioeconomic backgrounds.

Girls' overall sense of self-esteem at all-girls schools is roughly similar to girls' overall sense of self-esteem in co-educational environments. Considering Cairns' finding with middle school girls, the most likely conclusion is that girls at all-girls and co-educational schools achieve their self-worth through different avenues. Consistent with this notion, Granleese and Joseph (1993) found that girls at mixed-sex schools achieved their sense of self-worth primarily from their physical appearance, whereas the sense of self-worth of girls at single-sex schools appeared to be driven by their own behavioural conduct.

6

Gender and Perceived
Internet Efficacy

This chapter provides a critical discussion and empirical investigation of secondary digital divide factors, including gendered variations in Internet use. Analyses were conducted on data obtained from 716 respondents, who were self-reported Internet users based on a nation-wide telephone survey in Singapore. Results showed that females and males differed significantly in terms of their perceived Internet efficacy and identified various factors including socio-economic status, perceived Internet efficacy, and gender that undergird Internet use.

Concerns about informational inequities have been raised over the last two decades following the proliferation of the Internet and other web-based technologies. In the background of globalization and an increased dependency on digital products, services, and communications, Internet access and use has become pertinent for economic growth, political participation, and social inclusion. In the United States, the "digital divide" has emerged as the lingua franca encapsulating much research in the stratification patterns and inequalities relating to Internet adoption and use.

However, Miller (2001) notes that studies in other industrial societies are needed to illuminate the international variations in stratification processes that underlie the use of information technology, as the term digital divide is often used within a purely U.S.-centric context, referring specifically to the disparities in access to information and the growing underclass on the North American continent. The nature and scope of the digital divide is dependent on various measurement indices, which differ between contexts and from country to country.

In recent years, a number of measures have been developed to benchmark Internet growth rates, including measures of Internet adoption rates and Internet bandwidth, individual frequency of access, time online, intensity, and centrality of use. For example, in the second phrase of World Summit of Information Society at Tunis, a report of core ICT (information and communication technology) indicators for development comprehensively documented indices for ICT infrastructure, use of ICT by businesses, households, and individuals, and trade in ICT goods.

In South East Asia, the measurement of Internet access is dependent on estimates and sometimes difficulties in obtaining complete information about telephone and Internet subscription rates in developing regions, while Internet growth rates in terms of Internet subscribers and cable capacity in the relatively more developed nations including Singapore, Hong Kong, Japan, and South Korea have been closely tracked and reported in books by key Internet scholars.

Although past studies have highlighted the role of gender as one facet of the digital divide, more recent reports seem to sideline the importance of gender. This position is supported by the apparent increasing Internet adoption rates among both males and females as publicized in prominent telecommunications reports, such as the U.S. Department of Commerce (2002) report entitled "A Nation Online." Yet it is important to track gender differences in Internet usage after adoption because structural disparities may endure to produce deepening gaps and relative inequalities in Internet use. Groups that have lower usage rates risk being excluded from job and educational opportunities as well as losing political influence as the Internet becomes increasingly important to how people live and work.

This chapter examines the nature of the digital divide in Singapore, particularly in regard to the relationships between gender and Internet efficacy. This research focuses on the secondary digital divide concerning Internet use at home and at work, rather than the primary divide of Internet adoption due to the pervasive adoption of the Internet in Singapore. In the last decade, the Singapore government has aggressively embarked on various policies to build upon its role as an international, financial, and transportation hub by developing an advanced telecommunications infrastructure to support an increasingly sophisticated digital economy.

Tan (1998) attributes the rapid growth and adoption of the Internet in Singapore to a unique supply push and demand pull framework of technology. Government activity simultaneously creates the stimuli in the production and transfers of technology (the supply push) as well as provides the incentives for technology adoption (demand pull). In part as a consequence of strong leadership and community intervention, Singapore has been amongst the earliest and most vigorous adopters of the Internet.

According to recent statistics updated in December 2005, Singapore has one of the highest Internet penetration rates (67 per cent) in the world. More than two-thirds of the population in Singapore has adopted the Internet, a proportion comparable to the United States and Canada, and higher than the United Kingdom and many other countries in the European Union.

Hence, there is a popular consensus that the digital divide has been successfully bridged due to government and market forces. Singapore appears to have done so remarkably well in bridging the primary access divide that the government has come to redefine the digital divide as those who are Internet savvy and those who are not. However, the role and influence of gender in digital inequalities has received scarce attention despite traditional gendered stratification along socio-economic lines in a male-dominated, communitarian society where "Asian values" are prized for economic development.

Given that Singapore is ahead of many areas in the world in terms of Internet adoption and use, this context provides an interesting social laboratory for the examination of the secondary digital divide after initial Internet access has been achieved in many rapidly developing countries. Moreover, the case of Singapore may be instructive of how gender and other demographic and socio-psychological variables individually and collectively contribute to deepening the secondary digital divides in other developed and industrialized nations.

This chapter is organized as follows. First, the paper examines the pertinent literatures with regard to the digital divide and, more specifically, the studies on the gender gap mostly conducted in the North American and European contexts. The paper then proceeds to discuss the social context of Singapore's Internet penetration and use.

As in other articles on the social implications of the Internet, the reference to the "Internet" in this chapter may refer to the technical infrastructure, the electronic network of networks that connects people and information through computers and other digital devices, and the general uses of the infrastructure, including the World Wide Web, email, and other online interactive spaces. Following the literature review, the chapter presents an analysis and discussion of the results from the findings of a nation-wide survey. Finally, the paper concludes with the limitations of the research and possible implications of the results for social theorists and policy makers.

GENDER AND SECONDARY DIGITAL DIVIDES

In light of the emergence of the "information society," the notion of the digital divide has percolated through the scholarly and public policy discussion among policy makers and academics, including various communication studies and media scholars. The "digital divide," as popularly discussed in the United States, harkens back to a binary concept of information "haves and have-nots" in the 1980s and the "information rich and the information poor" when personal computers were first introduced and installed into schools.

Research in digital divide issues echo the concerns expressed by earlier research on the "knowledge gap" theory which posits that as the flow of information on a given topic into a community increases, people from higher socio-economic status are in a better position to take advantage of that information compared to others, thus potentially leading to differential knowledge among social groups. According to Tichenor et al., socioeconomic status, knowledge, and social networks contribute to the widening knowledge gap, which enables existing power holders to maintain their privileged positions in society. Ettema and Kline later modified the knowledge gap hypothesis to include how motivations may play a part in media adoption, given individual differences in the perception and understanding of knowledge.

In recent developments (particularly in the European context), the concept of "e-inclusion" and "digital choice" is preferred over the "digital divide" as expressed in various discussions on "the Information Society" (for examples, see the series of papers published or supported by the Commission of the European Communities). At the first World Summit on the Information Society at Geneva 2003, national governments of the world declared a commitment "to build a people-centered, inclusive, and development oriented Information Society".

Inclusion is stressed as an overarching goal aligned with national and regional efforts orchestrated to improve digital literacy to ensure all citizens benefit from what is understood as necessary participation in the present knowledge-based society and economy. Coupled with inclusion is the idea of digital choice and opportunity to connect to information technologies under what is perceived to be favorable conditions of use.

As Dutton (2004) points out in the United Nations Educational, Scientific and Cultural Organization (UNESCO) publication Social Transformation in the Information Society, gaps in Internet use may be viewed as not wholly a matter of socioeconomic circumstances, but also as strategic choice, operating in the context of domestication processes of new technologies in the home and workplace. Males and females may seek to gain control over the Internet and use new technology and services in order to maintain their communicative power and capacity to control the structure of their public and private lives.

Despite the ongoing debate and attention to social stratification processes associated with new media, the problem of the digital divide has been dismissed by some as irrelevant in light of the contemporary trend of high penetration rates of the Internet in industrialized countries like the U.S. For some observers, the digital divide is a transitory glitch and will be closed in time due to market forces.

The last National Telecommunications and Information Administration (NTIA) report entitled "A Nation Online: How Americans are expanding their use of the Internet" triumphantly emphasized the demise of the digital divide, as statistics evidenced the growing use of new information technologies across geographic regions and demographic groups, including gender. Moreover, diffusion theory and the S-curve have historically provided insight into the processes of technological adoption, and may be interpreted as an optimistic framework for digital inclusion achieved by the temporal processes of complete diffusion of the Internet in society over time.

An alternative view is that the "digital divide" is deepening because digital inequalities are manifest in patterns of Internet use. Attewell's (2001) helpful distinction characterizes the varying degrees of this digital divide where the first divide concerns computer access and ownership while the second divide pertains to computer use and, more specifically, includes the "social differences in the ways computers are used at school and at home".

After a comprehensive review of the literature on Internet access and inequality, Hargittai, DiMaggio, Celeste, and Shafer (2004) recommend that future research on the digital divide examine inequalities on various levels including skill, autonomy of use, and variation in use. Specifically, Internet skills and information search efficacy have been identified as secondary digital divide factors that may influence patterns of Internet use. Related to this, recent studies highlight persistent and widening inequalities beyond initial Internet adoption, to post-adoption patterns of use as newer variants of digital inequality. Under a conceptualization of multi-layered access, gender is still a predictor in more fine-grained analyses of Internet use.

According to Van Dijk (2005), gender constitutes a part of the deepening digital divide as the relational, categorical pair of male-female is linked to particular patterns of access to temporal, material, mental, social, and cultural resources that are reinforced by social exclusion, exploitation, and control mechanisms that may perpetuate durable inequalities in linked online and offline milieus. The conceptualization of the adoption of the Internet as a process of diffusion over time has also been critiqued as being overly optimistic and mechanical by critical scholars who highlight the need to understand the role of motivation and the differences in masculine and feminine enthusiasms toward technology as a basis of engagement with the Internet.

To date, a few studies on the digital divide have focused on empirically examining the differences in Internet adoption and use between males and females, with survey studies mostly conducted in North American contexts. For instance, Bimber (2000) analyzed survey data on Internet users in America from 1996 to 1999 and found that a statistically significant gender gap exists in terms of Internet use. His analysis showed that gender influenced use of the Internet as women are less likely than men to use the Internet frequently, when factors like employment rates and education are taken into account.

Another analysis of data from three large North American national surveys found that women are less-intensive Internet users and use the Internet more for social, rather than instrumental or recreational reasons. Most recently, research by the Pew Internet and America Life project published in 2005 found that since 2000, men and women do not differ in terms of their Internet access but to date still differ in the patterns of their Internet use and activities online.

On a typical day, wired men are more likely than wired women to go online. Results showed that 44% of men go online at least several times a day, compared with 39% of women (Fallows, 2005). Hence, results from prior studies suggest that although the gender gap in terms of access is disappearing at least in the North American context, gender is germane to secondary digital divide issues. However, the influence of gender-specific phenomena on Internet use is still unclear, as prior studies mainly center on examining differences in the patterns of Internet use between the sexes. Less attention has been paid to examining the associations between gender, and skill-based and social-psychological factors on Internet use.

GENDER AND PERCEIVED INTERNET EFFICACY

Communication and information technology research in the field of management science highlights the salience of self-efficacy factors in affecting technological adoption and use. For example, based on Bandura's social cognitive research on self-efficacy, Eastin & Larose discuss the concept of Internet efficacy, or "the belief in one's capabilities to organize and execute courses of Internet actions required to produce given attainments, as a potentially important factor in efforts to close the digital divide that separates experienced Internet users from novices".

Research related to perceived Internet efficacy points out that perceived Internet expertise is positively associated with the adoption and acceptance of certain technologies, including computing and Internet-related practices. Studies related to the technology acceptance model highlight the causal linkages between perceived ease of use, users' attitude, actual system adoption, and use. According to Eachus & Cassidy, web users' self-efficacy beliefs are influential for computer and Internet use among college students within the context of e-learning.

Furthermore, research in the development of a "computer-email and web fluency scale" to assess self-perceptions of web, computer, and email skills highlight that peoples' perceived aptitude to use the Internet and related technologies function as prerequisite technological skills and confidence needed to ameliorate the multidimensional nature of the digital divide.

Hence, the confidence in one's ability to use technology and one's expectations of the usefulness of the technology may constrain or facilitate one's online behaviours. However, gender has received little attention in technological adoption and other information technology (IT) diffusion research, although historically, research in the field of computing has found that males have more favorable attitudes towards computers and are less likely to be computer phobic than females.

Moreover, recent publications in the field of cyberpsychology generally test the relationships between gender, Internet-related attitudes, and Internet use among limited samples or college students. For example, a study conducted on undergraduate college students in America found that females reported higher levels of incompetence and discomfort with computers and the Internet than males. Results showed that competence and comfort levels with computers and the Internet were highly intercorrelated, and both predicted Internet skills and experiences.

Another study investigated gender, Internet identity, and Internet anxiety among college students in the United Kingdom. Results uncovered gender differences in students' use of the Internet, but it was found that females did not use the Internet for communication more than men. Further, there was a significant negative relationship between Internet anxiety and use of the Internet, although the contribution of gender to Internet use was found to be marginal after other demographic factors were accounted for. Thus, prior research points to the salience of individual perceptions towards technology on Internet use, though more research is needed to further clarify the socio-psychological mechanisms that affect the gender gaps online.

THE DIGITAL DIVIDE IN SINGAPORE

In the context of Singapore, many government regulations have historically shaped the contours of civil society, including the role of the Internet and the general public sphere. The Internet in Singapore coexists with the already established context of older media and lies in the intersection of various historical and social forces. Since the early 1980s, the Singapore government has been actively building a digital infrastructure and vigorously promoting the adoption and use of the Internet in people's everyday lives.

In an effort to boost its economic structure, the government has embarked on a concerted strategy to harness information technology for nation building. For example, consecutive national visions and master plans have been formulated to provide direction for the development and importance of the Internet in Singapore. These plans include the "National Computerization Plan", formation of the National Computer Board, the National Information Technology Plan, "A Vision of an Intelligent Island", and the "IT2000 Masterplan," which accompanied the launch of a nation-wide broadband high-speed network.

The latest plans include "Infocomm21: Infocomm Capital" and "Connected Singapore" (2003 to present), which focuses on improving all aspects of the e-economy and e-society. With regard to the development of digital literacy, the Ministry of Education laid out a "Masterplan for IT" in 1997 to provide a blueprint for the use of IT in schools and access to an IT-enriched school environment for every Singaporean student.

The plan, in tandem with the Ministry of Education's "thinking schools, learning nation" initiative, aimed to provide one computer for every two pupils from Primary one (elementary) to junior college (pre-university), for students to use IT for 30% of their curriculum time and for all teachers to have email accounts.

Various other nation-wide initiatives have also been organized to raise the adoption of the Internet, including year-long "e-celebration" festivals organized by the Infocomm Development Authority of Singapore, where information technology exhibitions are held and activities are organized to provide free computing and Internet training. In light of the dominant agenda of nation-building and economic progress, the Internet is framed within the rubric of scientific progress and the development of a new information economy.

Consequently, in many ways individual attitudes and perceptions toward technology may play a relatively significant role in influencing Internet use since primary access is fast becoming commonplace due to aggressive, state-led efforts to wire up the country. In spite of this, research into secondary digital divide issues has been eclipsed in light of the popular belief held by various public policy and industry leaders that digital inequalities have been successfully bridged in Singapore; an enviable predicament compared to Singapore's less industrialized and prosperous neighbors in the Asian region.

The image of Singapore as an "e-city" has also been reinforced by reports recognizing Singapore as a model case study example of digital inclusivity (for example, The United Nations International Telecommunications Union's (2001) case study report on Singapore). Furthermore, in a keynote address at the Institute of Policy Studies entitled "The Digital Divide in Asia and the World: Opportunities and Challenges," it was noted that:

Here in Singapore, the divide is almost invisible. Thanks to the brilliant development of the country over the last four decades, Singapore is now prosperous, well wired states, where almost all citizens live on the right side of the digital divide ... Singapore, then, is fully integrated in the digital world.

More importantly, the role of gender in digital inequalities has been overlooked in spite of traditional social stratification along gender lines. This research lacuna is of serious concern, as several studies have highlighted that although greater parity has occurred in the last two decades, substantial divisions in terms of income, education, and occupational status remain among males and females in Singapore. Feminist theory suggests that a woman's career in information technology is socially structured and past studies highlight the role of the government, the structure of family and peer groups, and conflict between household responsibilities and job demands, which discourage women from pursuing leadership in their work or retaining professional roles in the economy.

Local sociologists also note that Singapore appears to be very "western" and egalitarian in many aspects, but gendered differences in cultural and social norms exist akin to other traditional male-dominated Asian societies operant according to Confucian ideology. In many areas, submissiveness to males is favored in the public and private spheres in line with patriarchal mindsets toward social governance and political leadership. Females have historically been (and still remain) significantly underrepresented in government and parliament.

Furthermore, overt government economic wage-earning and childbearing incentive policies, as well as more covert forms of social control, have reinforced perceptions of the subordinate position of females in the home and in the workplace; even though meritocracy is espoused and educational opportunities have risen for women in the last two decades. Systematic discourse in both public and private domains stresses male dominance and self-identification along a range of acceptable female life experiences like domestic affairs, "nonscientific" knowledge, and religious rituals control.

Set up in 1985, the group Association of Women for Action and Research (AWARE), is the first and only advocacy group dedicated to promoting gender equality and understanding of gender biases, particularly prejudices and discrimination against professional women in high-status, high-wage occupations traditionally dominated by men. In sum, prior digital divide research suggests that inequities in terms of Internet use exist, although access gaps are closing in many industrialized nations.

Past conceptualizations of the digital divide have segregated people into heavy and light users based on time spent online. However, little research has comprehensively examined the relationships between gender and Internet efficacy factors that affect Internet use. Furthermore, gender inequalities online have been unexplored within Internet studies in Singapore. Hence, this study investigates whether or not difference exists in Internet use along gender lines in Singapore and asks the following inter-related questions: (a. What differences exist in the perceived Internet efficacy of female and male Internet users?, and (b. In what ways and to what extent do gender, demographics, and perceived Internet efficacy individually and/or collectively affect Internet use?

Data for this study were obtained from a nation-wide survey conducted under the auspices of the Singapore Internet Research Center, Nanyang Technological University, in which data on Internet use, perceived Internet efficacy, social attitudes, and religion were collected in November 2004. The questionnaire was administered via a Computer Assisted Telephone Interviewing (CATI) system with interviews conducted in English. Respondents were screened for both citizenship and Internet use.

A probability sample was obtained by generating random numbers, and then randomizing respondents within each household. At least eight attempts were made to complete an interview at every household that was included in the sample. Respondents who refused to participate were re-contacted a maximum of two more times to persuade them to complete the interview. Calls were made from 4:00 to 10:00 p.m. over 6 days by trained interviewers. This procedure produced a response rate of 57% and resulted in 716 completed surveys.

The survey instrument contained questions on perceived Internet efficacy, Internet use, and socio-demographic factors. Respondents were asked to rate their levels of agreement with four statements on perceived Internet efficacy, specifically regarding their confidence in describing, using, and trouble-shooting Internet hardware and software. These four items were taken from a general eight-item scale on Internet self-efficacy created specifically to better understand the psychology of the digital divide. Statements included, "You feel confident understanding terms or words related to Internet hardware," "You feel confident understanding terms or words relating to Internet software," "You feel confident describing functions of Internet hardware," and "You feel confident trouble shooting Internet problems."

Responses were measured on a 1 to 7 Likert scale of agreement and were reverse coded, with the highest value indicating a very strong agreement with the statements. A principal components analysis with varimax rotation yielded a single factor with an eigen-value of 2.5 and explaining 62.5% of the variance. The Cronbach's alpha for the scale was acceptably high at .80. Internet use was measured by asking the respondents if and how frequently they use the Internet at work/school and at home.

For the two questions on Internet use at work and at home, response categories were grouped into six categories, with "1" indicating "never," "2" indicating "every few weeks or less often," "3" indicating "1-2 days a week," "4" indicating "3-5 days a week," "5" indicating "about once a day," and "6" indicating "several times a day."

Socio-demographic factors, including gender, age, income, education, race, and marital status, were used in the analyses. Respondents were asked their age on their last birthday. Education was measured by a single item, "education level of respondent," and was categorized into four levels from "some secondary and below" (equivalent to less than a middle school education) to "college level and above." Income was measured by total gross family income per month and was categorized into 4 levels from $2,000 or less (equivalent to US$1,250 or less) and "above $6,000" (equivalent to US$3,700 or more). Race was coded as "1" for Chinese (predominant race of the population) and "0" for non-Chinese.

Of the 716 respondents, 374 (52%) were male and 342 (48%) were female. Respondents ranged in age from 19 to 89 with a mean age of 33. Twenty-seven per cent received less than a high school education, 46% attained a high school education and above, and 27% received at least a college degree. Respondents' monthly household income ranged from less than $2,000 to above $6,000, with a median monthly household income in the range of $2,000 to $4,000. Seventy-nine per cent of the population were Chinese and 51% of the respondents were married.

This survey targeted Internet users only, so there were several differences between the sample and the general population as reported in the last national Census 2000. For example, Internet users tended to be younger than the population at large. Specifically, the sample had a much larger number of respondents in the 18-24 age range (31%) than was found in the last census (12%) and a much smaller number of respondents from the 65 and above category (1.3%) compared to the census results (7.3%).

There were also slightly more male respondents in the sample (52%) than in the general population of Singapore (50%). In terms of race, there were about an equal proportion of Chinese respondents (79%), and less from those of other Malay (11%) and Indian (4%) races in the sample than in the population census (14% and 8%, respectively). These demographic differences reflect another aspect of the primary digital divide in terms of Internet access. With regard to Internet use at work/school, 34% use it several times a day, 20% use it about once a day, 8% use it 3-5 days a week, 8% use it 1-2 days a week, 11% use it once every few weeks or less often, and 20% do not use it at all.

With regard to Internet use at home, 24% of the respondents use it several times a day, 27% use it about once a day, 15% use it 3-5 days a week, 16% use it 1-2 days a week, 11% use it once every few weeks or less often, and 7% do not use it at all. Among the respondents, relationships between perceived Internet efficacy, Internet use at home, and Internet use at home were positive. Correlations between the variables were small, ranging from .16 to .21. Respondents who rated themselves as more efficacious with the Internet also tended to be younger, Chinese, more educated, single, and male.

GENDERED DIFFERENCES IN PERCEIVED INTERNET EFFICACY

The first research question sought to investigate if there were any gender differences in respondents' perceived Internet efficacy. Results showed significant gender differences in the proportion of males and females who were confident of their Internet expertise. Findings showed that on all four statements on Internet efficacy, males rated themselves higher than females. Specifically, males were significantly more likely to rate themselves to be more confident in understanding terms or words related to Internet hardware and software, in describing functions of Internet hardware and in trouble-shooting Internet problems.

FACTORS AFFECTING INTERNET USE

The second question of the study was to examine the extent to which gender and other socio-psychological factors individually and collectively predicted Internet use at work/school and at home. Stepwise hierarchical multiple regression analysis was used to control for intercorrelations and to better identify the unique variance explained by each block of variables. Block one contained the demographic variables age, income, education, race, and marital status. Block two contained the perceived Internet efficacy factor. Block three contained the gender variable.

Data revealed that income, education, and marital status were significantly related to Internet use. Age and race were not related to Internet use at work/school. Those who were single and had a higher income and education were more likely to use the Internet more frequently. Findings of the second regression analysis showed that perceived Internet efficacy was a significant predictor of individuals' Internet use after the effects of individual demographics were controlled.

Results showed that those who considered themselves to be confident of their Internet use capabilities were more likely to use the Internet more frequently. Findings of the third regression analysis showed that, over and above the effects of individual demographics and Internet efficacy, gender was a significant predictor of individuals' Internet use. Findings showed that females tended to use the Internet less intensively than their male counterparts, after other demographic variables and perceived Internet efficacy were controlled.

With regard to Internet use at home, a similar pattern of results emerged, with slight differences. Results showed that that those who were younger, single, and had a higher income and education were more likely to use the Internet more frequently at home. In addition, results from the second regression showed that over and above the effects of individual demographics, perceived Internet efficacy was a significant predictor of individuals' Internet use at home.

Results showed that those who considered themselves to be confident of their Internet use capabilities were more likely to use the Internet more frequently at home. Findings from the third regression analysis showed that females tended to use the Internet less frequently than their male counterparts after socio-economic status variables and perceived Internet efficacy were controlled.

The Internet possesses great potential to improve the social participation and economic well being of traditionally marginalized and disadvantaged groups, including females, in many countries. However, considerable barriers to Internet access and use exist, which may portend a looming information gap between those who access and use the Internet efficaciously and those who do not. This study set out to discuss and explore the area of research and debate on the secondary digital divide issues within the Singaporean context.

Specifically, it examined the relationships between gender, socio-economic status, perceived Internet efficacy, and Internet use among Internet users in order to illuminate the patterns of gendered variations underlying Internet use at work and at home. Results from a nation-wide survey showed that females and males differed significantly in terms of their perceived Internet efficacy, with the same gender variation found in earlier studies in computer adoption and technology use in Anglophone contexts.

One reason why females tend to perceive themselves as less efficacious may be that women tend to underrate their abilities in comparison to men's self-rating and to third-party assessments as highlighted in prior psychological research. Past research related to self-efficacy in fields of child development and sociology have indicated that in general, males have a greater sense of self-efficacy, personal control, and mastery than do females. The most common explanations for these differences involve cultural factors like sex-role stereotypes and the structural social environments of males and females.

Specifically in Singapore, a culture-related reason why females tend to perceive themselves as less efficacious in terms of Internet use may be the influence of Asian/Confucian values where females are oftentimes viewed in a subordinate position and may claim expertise only in certain socially acceptable practices apart from professional technical or engineering fields.

In addition, Internet use has been recently promoted as the key path for economic growth and national development in Singapore and other key Asian economies and, thus, may be more strongly associated with high-status and high-wage labour positions that traditionally have been dominated by males. Hence, in spite of the modernization of Singapore, results of this study suggest that feminism and equalization of gender are incomplete and have not completely succeeded in changing dominant social attitudes in ways that accommodate changed practices in terms of technological use.

Perversely, modernization may have merely stimulated Internet access for both males and females but some social categories, like men, may still be using and benefiting more from the so-called information revolution. Indeed, findings from the two sets of regression analyses show the presence of secondary digital divides after initial Internet access. Results show that gender, age, marital status, income, education, as well as perceived Internet efficacy significantly affected Internet use at work and at home in Singapore. Respondents who were males, single, and of higher income and education were also more likely to use the Internet frequently.

In this aspect, results here have implications for Internet research as findings highlight the importance of investigating secondary digital divide issues, particularly Internet use after initial access is achieved. It is commonly believed among policy makers and community leaders that promoting information technologies is key to achieving social inclusion among urban populations. Yet, ironically, social fragmentation could be furthered by arguably ubiquitous Internet access.

As Jan Van Dijk (2005) astutely observed about durable inequalities associated with Internet use, "the digital divide is deepening where it has stopped widening". Therefore, it is pertinent that results here illustrate how demographic and socio-economic variables may still be relevant for post-Internet adoption behaviours like Internet use in the context of Singapore and other industrialized nations where the Internet is reaching maturity and growth rates are stabilizing.

Interestingly, the contribution of gender per se to Internet use, after controlling for other demographic variables and perceived Internet efficacy, was found to be significant but relatively marginal in both models. Given the traditional gender stratification in income and education in Singapore, it appears that gender may act as a proxy variable for socioeconomic status to some extent. Having stated this, it is important to note that the females feel that they lack Internet expertise while at the same time they report significantly less frequent use of the Internet, suggesting an interaction effect between technological attitudes and system use that will not be easily disentangled.

Specifically, regression analyses showed that gender differences in Internet use were in part accounted for by differences in perceived Internet efficacy, but still exerted a significant effect after socio-economic status and perceived Internet efficacy was controlled, suggesting that other gender-related mechanisms are at work. Thus, gender-related inequalities in Internet use cannot be explained by income or educational barriers alone, as they may reflect differential attitudes towards the Internet and possibly a range of domestication processes by females in their homes and workplaces as they attempt to alter their communicative power or maintain the existing structures of their everyday lives.

LIMITATIONS AND FUTURE RESEARCH CONSIDERATIONS

It is acknowledged that several limitations exist. First, survey data from this study represent a single, cross-sectional snapshot of Internet use. Thus, any ability to draw causal inferences and overtime observations on the relationships among study factors is impossible. Second, measurement of perceived Internet efficacy is based on self-reported measures.

According to Eachus & Cassidy (2004), the nature of self-efficacy is usually measured using self-report scales as it is an ego-centric construct. However, future studies could extend the inquiry into this critical study factor by direct observations of Internet efficacy to include more comprehensive measures that focus on specific types of Internet behaviour or evaluation of searches of certain domain-specific information online.

Third, occupational variables were not included as covariates in the analyses as data were unavailable. Future research should extend digital divide research by incorporating occupational variables. For example, Losh (2004) found that gender differences in IT access and use lessened when labour force participation was controlled. It is worth noting that the current study provides measures of Internet use in two important locales, at work/school and at home. However, it may be the case that females experience limitations on their time and use of the Internet in these spaces.

For example, a case study on 30 Anglo-Celtic women in Australia found gender differences in the use of the Internet at home, as seen from the women's perspectives. In addition, as the Internet coexists and competes with other media for one's attention, spending less time online may be a rational management strategy for females' everyday lives, rather than a problematic demonstration of their poorer digital connections. Hence, future research on secondary digital divides could incorporate qualitative data collected via other strategies like interviews, observational studies, and focus groups to complement quantitative data on Internet use to provide more in-depth illustrations of how the social, symbolic, and individual dimensions of gender interact with daily uses and interpretation of the Internet.

Finally, this research on secondary digital divides focused on an aspect of Internet use of Internet users, as data on other measures of online activities, including the centrality of the Internet in one's everyday life, were not collected in this study.

Future studies could extend this investigation to include activities online, for example, specific feminist uses of IT in Singapore and to what ends females use information accessed online.

The discussion and findings in this chapter are important for communication professionals, social activists, and policy makers who are interested in studying social stratification and potentially affecting changes to promote gender equity in terms of digital access and use. The study uses data taken from a nation-wide sample of Internet users and provides illustrations of the various social and psychological factors pertinent to secondary digital divide in industrialized countries. Similar to the policy implications drawn from a growing body of research on gender gaps online, these findings highlight the need for targeted and integrated efforts that are aligned with other social inclusion policies that reach out to the poorer, less educated, and female segments of the population to boost their confidence and expertise in Internet use.

Furthermore, the current data provide a more complete picture of the gender gaps online. Clearly, examining the relationship between gender and Internet use is incomplete when limiting the focus to only gendered differences in Internet use. Just as important are demographic, attitudinal, and capability factors, such as perceived Internet efficacy, which may contribute to widening or mitigating the digital divide, given that confidence building can be a vital link between enhanced digital and social inclusion.

Finally, in many ways, the Asian economic growth miracle and, more recently, the information societies of Asia, including Japan, South Korea, Taiwan, and Singapore, have received much international publicity as networked societies and have been promoted as technological leaders and innovators with an advanced Internet infrastructure. Thus, it is important to qualify that secondary digital divides exists even in cities where apparent digital inclusivity have been achieved and what appears to be the new optimism observed about the closing of the gender divide.

Results here suggest that modernization in terms of telecommunications infrastructure and production of technological hardware does not equate to digital and social equity. Social hierarchy and attitudes towards technology may be established in subtle but impressive ways.

Digital divide and communication theorists should be cognizant of the meanings and realities of connectivity for females who are poorer, married, and are less educated as governments attempt to create 'e-societies' and promote equitable digital living in both work and home environments. The digital divide phenomenon continues to be an important issue in many parts of the world and a deepened understanding would illuminate gendered differences and social variation that undergird evolving contemporary societies' increasing dependence on information and communication technologies.

7

Gendered IT
From Digital Binary to Analog Continuum

Technology is more than just objects. Technology is, as Ursula Franklin suggests in her germinal work, The Real World of Technology, also a set of social practices and processes that define communities and groups through "ways of doing something." Terms such as "knowledge economy" and "information worker" define a group of immensely diverse occupations and industries by their shared "way of doing something," namely, working with information technologies (IT).

Though these terms are used primarily as labels that delineate highly valued groups, they also often conceal, rather than reveal, the nature of such work. Is a data entry worker, for example, an "information worker" in the same way as a software designer, because they both use a computer to process information? The definitions of such occupational groups can also lead to particular assumptions of value about the work. We tend not to ask what is actually "known" in our "knowledge economy," or for that matter, whether "knowing" is better than "understanding."

The use of the word "knowledge" is peculiar in this case, as the ultimate goal of many technological systems is to eliminate human error and presumed user stupidity. Other types of occupations not viewed as "knowledge occupations," such as trades occupations, can be comparatively rich in knowledge, expertise, and critical tidbits of data. Given that in the context of scientific rationalism, certain marginalized groups of people, including women, have not been viewed as "knowers" and have been excluded from particular kinds of knowledge communities, such terms can hide the social relations of power and privilege that shape technological processes.

All forms of work have been affected by technology. Technological developments have changed what is seen as normal, possible, and desirable. Although all forms of work have been changed by technology, they tend to retain the structure that was present before the technology was introduced. For example, despite the introduction of a wide variety of household technologies, women still do the bulk of unpaid domestic labour in the home. While indeed it takes longer to learn to use a cyclotron than to use a vacuum cleaner, the fact remains that while technology has in some way altered all forms of work, it has tended not to change the social relations upon which work is premised.

"Knowledge work" or, more accurately, work within a field that is broadly labeled information technology (IT), has often been portrayed since the advent of the computer network as a fundamentally new form of work. While IT work has now become routine and, indeed, with the downturn of the so-called dotcom industry, something of a symbol of industrial hubris, there is nevertheless a pervasive cultural sense that despite such glitches of banality and imminent economic deflation the inevitable "progress" will nevertheless occur.

Industry publications are rife with panting hyperbole about the power of technology to change the world, even as they lament job losses to offshore programmers. Despite the IT industry's claim to novelty, considerable evidence exists that IT highlights ongoing tensions in the general organization of the labour market and evokes concerns around labour that have been familiar since the Industrial Revolution. Despite new language and new tasks, technological work reflects and reproduces fundamental social, economic, and political trends. In terms of the technology itself, social relations largely determine its conception, development, implementation, and process.

TECHNOLOGICAL LABOUR AND GENDER

Early work on technology and gender tended to homogenize both these elements. Certain assumptions were embedded in discussions of gender and technology. For example, "gender" usually meant "women" (and only a certain imagined group of women who stood for the collective whole of women), and "technology" meant "computers" and not, say, blenders or tampon applicators. Technological theories such as those of Sadie Plant took up the notion of "digital" as a metaphor for emergent technological practices, playing on the term as an expression of information technologies and the "binary" relations between women and men.

More recent theory suggests, however, that given the complexity of social relations, it is insufficient for us to theorize technological work using a limited binary framework of men versus women, creators and masters versus users. Indeed, much work has been done on the ways gender relations between and among men and women are constructed in IT-related work spheres. For example, the performance and organization of masculinity is a complex phenomenon in IT workplaces, with different types of masculinity emerging based on adherence to norms such as social organization, perceived skill types, and abilities.

Not only is gender a complicated, sometimes contradictory, and nuanced phenomenon. An examination of ways it is experienced in the larger workplace and, in particular, the IT-related workplaces, must also look at other dimensions of worker experience and stratification. These can include geographic location, perceived and actual skill levels, immigration status, and age. Thus, we must approach the research in a more complex way, using an intersectional approach which more precisely represents the diverse processes and practices of IT work.

Gender must be combined with indicators of other social location and conditions of work (such as employment form) to depict accurately the complexity of the technological work force and the implementation of technological labour practices. The experience of IT work thus resembles the continuum or spectrum of the analog, rather than the binary structure of the digital.

RELATIONS OF SKILL AND PRACTICE

Considerable attention is devoted to designating which work is "technical enough" to merit consideration as IT work. This designation is also inherently based on social relations. The term "skilled workers" is assumed to apply unproblematically to a clearly defined category of technologically competent workers. Yet it is evident that large numbers of workers who consistently employ technological skill to perform their position's duties are not counted in this group. Moreover, workers who do have a high degree of skill, such as skilled immigrants and particularly female immigrants of color, may find that their technical skills are not seen as valid when they arrive in such countries as Canada.

How "skill" is understood and valued and who has access to the skills that are required and valued depend on the social relations of power and privilege. In general terms, technologically facilitated work is understood to be more skilled, but in practice, there are strata of technological occupations and tasks whose value appears to depend heavily on existing relations of both gender and other elements of social location. For example, while technical personnel working in company IT departments are viewed as skilled, their job does not carry the professional designation, status, and compensation of traditional technoscientific occupations such as engineers or lab researchers.

Though both occupational groupings are coded as male, it's not sufficient simply to be a technically-skilled man; rather, skill is also evaluated in a context of social hierarchies that operate both within each field and in the larger occupational context. Second, it is apparent that the way technology is implemented and experienced as part of the labour process depends on existing structural relations.

The reorganization of work in the late twentieth and early twenty-first centuries, which brought restructuring, an increase in nonstandard labour, emphasis on worker mobility and "flexibility," and increasingly fluid transnational capital and production, provided a particular social and economic context for the development of technologically facilitated work.

In keeping with Ursula Franklin's observations about the standardization, fragmentation, and "procedurization" of the labour process, employer attention to total quality management (TQM), just-in-time (JIT) production techniques, and control over all elements of the labour process provided the drive for (and was fostered by) technological developments. Thus, technology fulfills both a descriptive and a prescriptive function: it emerges in response to existing demands, but it also helps to determine what is considered "normal" and desirable.

Immersed in social relations, the valuation of technological practice now plays a crucial role in determining which forms of work are seen as skilled and valuable. For example, in Canada, as part of the New Brunswick government's recruitment of call centers to the province, the "high-tech" industry and "knowledge economy" were clearly linked to call center work despite clear differences between their divergent types of work.

It was hoped that the discursive value assigned to "high-tech" work would transfer to call center work, erasing the profound disparities between ways these two types of work were performed, remunerated, and evaluated as well as by whom the work was performed. The call center industry, associated as it is with female-dominated, routine, low-paid, low-status labour, is not usually viewed as a technologically based profession and yet it is only made possible by the merger of information and telecommunications technology. This ideological exercise obscures the restructuring process that grounded the shift to call centers in the first place and created a discursive, if not actual, connection of this low-status, and low-paid work to elite high-tech firms.

OCCUPATIONAL HYBRIDITY

Feminist scholars in the field of technology studies have pointed to "hybridity" as a useful metaphor by which to theorize emergent forms of work in the new economy. Indeed, the concept of the cyborg, as introduced by Donna Haraway, has generated a body of feminist scholarship that uses the notions of border crossing and mixed identities as ideas representing a variety of feminist engagements with technology.

Though Haraway's original piece was, in part, explicitly about women's work, it has rarely been used to take up the material dimensions of IT employment, a factor that is particularly interesting, given that IT has indeed led to the development of new, hybrid occupations. Web designers, for example, combine elements of programming with elements of graphic design. Yet, in IT work, representing "occupational hybridity" has remained a difficult task, particularly at a time when nonstandard forms of work are growing.

Occupational hybridity in practical terms is multilayered, variously experienced, and, in many cases, merely a promotional label for work processes that remains unchanged but is increasingly subject to deregulation. Additionally, reports of the death of old work styles and arrangements are greatly exaggerated, and new language barely conceals the fact that in many ways, technologically assisted forms of work emulate the practices of a century ago.

The discourse about "new" and "progressive," common in the work of futurist writers such as Alvin Toffler and Nicolas Negroponte, rejects an imagined past in favour of a technologically empowered future, but these assumptions of novelty have remained underexamined. For example, the idea of "flexibility" enjoys heavy rotation in technocratic circles. The presumed "newness" of this idea, and its links to IT, have been taken for granted, and there has been "no discussion on the origins of the term, to so that analysts may unravel its many connotations, to question what is indeed 'new,' and to set this more detailed analysis against the ideological processes that have unleashed it."

More cynical writers on the concept of labour flexibility note sardonically that the labour of marginalized groups such as women and workers of color has always been "flexible" or, more truthfully, piecemeal, cobbled together, insecure, with women's working time snatched from the jaws of domestic and other demands. Occupational hybridity operates on at least two levels. First, there is hybridity at the level of the work process, which usually includes the synthesis of different types of tasks and skills, especially those types of tasks and skills associated with disparate occupations. I have already mentioned Web designers.

Another example is technical writers, who must combine an ability to write well and clearly with in-depth knowledge of the technological object or process they are writing about. Second, hybridity creeps in at the level of work arrangements. Hybridity here includes changes to the hours, location, and manner of work-for example, combining work at home (connected to the workplace by e-mail, phone, fax, etc.) with work done on an employer's premises. It might also mean serving an employer in the capacity of an employee, but carrying the label of "independent contractor" or "self-employed."

These manifestations of hybridity, while facilitated by developments in IT, are also intimately linked to the proliferation of increasingly precarious and casual forms of employment (for example, part-time and temporary work). Attempts to measure occupational hybridity "objectively" and to see it only as a result of technological progress can obscure key trends that are part of globalized work restructuring, such as a move toward creation of precarious jobs held mostly by women. While technology itself indeed fosters new types of connections, it is not the only factor that changes (or doesn't change) the nature of work.

Hybridity is difficult to define because it is shorthand for a larger, more complex phenomenon and may serve ideological interests that deliberately obscure relations of power in structuring the labour market. Occupational hybridity can show us how labour processes in the "new" economy demonstrate increasing boundary-crossing in their task and skill requirements while demanding new forms of employment. During my PhD dissertation research, in which I interviewed female IT workers, I noted that subjects described occupational hybridity in their own work, such as the ability to synthesize apparently unrelated occupational demands through IT, and, as a result, create new types of jobs.

On the positive side, many women made inroads into formerly male-dominated technical arenas by creating new "crossover" IT work from formerly female-typed job categories, such as librarianship or publishing. Unfortunately, the status of these new jobs was often tenuous. Occupational hybridity in IT also often meant piecing together several jobs or contracts, often with limited duration or insecure conditions, for the woman worker to guarantee herself sufficient income.

One place to begin is to point out the disconnect between the multitasking or flexible labour of an IT worker, an increase in gendered precariousness in the labour market, and the rigidity of categorical tools and methods that are consequently unable to represent these relationships adequately. A researcher who attempts to use more traditional quantitative data may find that occupational classification systems used may be outdated. Additionally, focusing on creating "better" or "more accurate" classifications can obstruct important examinations of structural relations of power.

INDUSTRIAL AND OCCUPATIONAL CLASSIFICATION

Thus one of the central difficulties in empirical examination of IT work is the lack of adequate classification tools. IT work cuts across all industrial sectors and many occupational categories. Much of IT work thus becomes hidden; its being rendered invisible depends partially on social relations. Historically, technological work was closely associated with science, engineering, and medicine, and IT work continues to retain this connection despite other historical connections to clerical and applied design work and despite the widespread use of technological objects and practices across all domains.

Technoscientific fields have traditionally been linked to quite particular types of workers. It is not coincidental, then, that assumptions about IT work incorporate assumptions about who performs this work, and that work performed in traditionally nonwhite, non-male jobs is often viewed as less technical, regardless of the technological objects that are employed in the process.

Although, for example, Web designers are considered IT workers, clerical workers who do Web design as part of their administrative responsibilities are not. On the other hand, work that is "just technical" is increasingly performed by workers outside of North America and Europe. Programmers, for example, who used to enjoy substantial job status, are now more likely to be found in India making a third of North American wages. Data entry clerks who spend their entire shift with a computer are dispersed throughout low-income regions such as the Caribbean, though they may be viewed locally as semi-professional office workers.

The North American factory worker who performs the precise craft of electronics manufacturing, assembling the circuitry that high-status IT workers require, is likely to be a relatively low-paid immigrant woman of color. Thus, the examination of technological work, particularly its gendered nature, cannot be reduced to an occupational classification alone. However, traditional analyses have often relied on this technique, eliding issues of how technological occupations are valued, understood, practiced, and incorporated into a larger social context.

Occupational and industrial classification by statistical agencies, such as the NOC-S or NAICS used by Statistics Canada, is often viewed as a definitive measurement of empirical accuracy. Yet it is clear that statistical categories are fraught with problems. They can carry ideological baggage with them. Moreover, what is absent made invisible or not measured by empirical data and taxonomies may be as significant as what is present. For example, the absence of women's paid and unpaid work in conventional measurements of economic productivity was a subject of much concern for feminist economists.

Categorization may not accurately reflect how gendered technological work is understood in other fields, such as feminist sociology or political economy. It may not adequately represent work that is actually being done. Empirical classification is often slow to catch up to rapid shifts in work practice. Given that technology is defined primarily by its practice, such a taxing complexity becomes significant. Categorization may also hide shifts in work that are part of a deliberate agenda to downgrade, deskill, or restructure jobs.

As feminist scholars, we need nuanced tools for understanding IT work, particularly in the current socioeconomic context of an increasing precariousness of employment that may be obscured by pro-technological rhetoric. Qualitative data provides us with an entry point because such data show that limiting analysis to industrial and occupational classification is insufficient. The literature on gender and technology, as well as on the feminization of employment, also highlights a tension between noting persistently gendered trends in the organization of work, and reducing work experiences to gender alone.

Our project is twofold: we must expand and interrogate the classification of IT labour, combining it with various indicators such as social location, geography, and the temporal-spatial nature of work. The final section of this chapter will look at these factors, which can contribute to creating a multidimensional picture of ways the gender relations of IT work are deployed.

INDICATORS OF TECHNOLOGICAL WORK

One approach for understanding the heterogeneous yet persistently gendered relations of IT work is an intersectional one, which identifies numerous indicators and dimensions that are significant to but not determining of ways IT work is experienced. In other words, what factors combine to shape people's IT work narratives?

How can we develop a complex, nuanced picture of the current state of IT work in Canada, which recognizes the role of structural relations and employment arrangements and which retains structure but allows for diversity? The following are indicators of technological work that should be considered when developing a multi-dimensional analysis of the technological workforce.

INDICATORS OF THE EMPLOYMENT RELATIONSHIP

The "employment relationship" is an expression of how a worker is situated in relation to her wage-earning activities. Indicators of the employment relationship are significant in that they enable a more complex portrait of the IT labour force. For example, in their study of the call center industry, Buchanan and Koch-Schulte point out that wages and job security depend heavily on form of employment: full-time versus part-time, temporary versus permanent or even officially employed versus "independent contractor" or casual worker.

Significant shifts have occurred in the IT labour market in the past ten years. In particular, many employees have been reclassified as "self-employed" despite the fact that their relationship to one employer has not changed much. Many women have opted for part-time work, facilitated by IT, to meet the demands of their domestic responsibilities.

However, in many IT occupations that are under economic threat, this "choice" carries with it a penalty of outmoded skills, lost income, and perhaps greater employment precariousness. The question of precariousness is also key when noting that IT occupations tend not to enjoy regulatory protections such as collective agreements. Such protections have been key for women in ensuring that they attain adequate wages and benefits. Thus, an account of gender relations within IT must take into account the variant forms of employment and their gendered effects on IT workers.

1. Class of worker
    a. Employee
    b. Self-employed
2. Form of employment
    a. Part-time
    b. Full-time

3. Job permanency
   a.   Permanent
   b.   Temporary (this category can be further broken down into casual, seasonal, and temporary work through agencies)
4. Degree of regulatory protection
   a.   Coverage by a collective agreement

INDICATORS OF SOCIAL LOCATION

"Social location" positions elements such as gender, race, immigrant status, and so forth as a sort of "place" where relations of social, economic, and political power intersect to influence people's experiences. Gender has been a key social location in studies of IT work, but other social locations have remained undertheorized, except as occasional cultural signifiers.

Very little theory has dealt with elements such as age, ability or disability, and immigrant status, for example. Yet, research on workplace stratification clearly demonstrates the role that social location plays in determining outcomes such as earnings and occupational mobility. IT work appears to be no exception.

Examining social location as a major factor in IT workplace organization can be very useful, particularly when factors are combined. For example, it is important to combine immigrant status with so-called "visible minority" status, ethnic background, and country of origin. The workplace trajectory of a white Anglophone American IT worker who has immigrated to Canada is likely to be somewhat different from that of a worker of color from Somalia. The picture is further enriched by layering gender atop the elements of immigrant status.

Indicators of Social Location:

1. Gender
2. Age
3. Immigrant
4. Visible minority
5. Ethnic background
6. Ability and activity limitations

INDICATORS OF SKILL

What work is viewed as "skilled" depends, in part, on who is assumed to perform it. Women and workers from many marginalized groups are assumed to be less skilled than other workers such as white men (and occasionally, men of visibly Asian ethnicities). Interestingly, unlike many professions, IT employers often privilege youth and "hipness" in their skill judgments. Older workers who normally might enjoy career seniority are often viewed as not "cutting-edge" enough to compete or unable to accommodate rapidly changing skill demands.

Despite this perception, however, younger workers are, on average, paid less. In addition, employer requirements for demonstrated skills expertise are increasing, and documentation of "skill" in IT work is becoming increasingly institutionalized. Demand for formal, private credentials such as MCSE (Microsoft Certified Systems Engineer) is increasing among employers. Similarly, private, often poorly regulated skills instruction that actively recruits immigrants with the promise of a fast ticket to a good Canadian job is proliferating.

Thus, formal indicators of skill, such as educational attainment, should not be regarded as fully determinant of IT workers' experiences. What skills are possessed is, indeed, important, but the perception of skill possession is also demonstrably significant.

Indicators of Skill:

1. Educational attainment
2. Credentials (esp. Private, commercial certifications)
3. Experience
4. Informal learning

TIME AND PLACE OF WORK

Time and place of work are particularly significant for technological labour because of the geographical and temporal mobility that technology enables and because of the ideological role of concepts like "cyberspace" and "asynchronous work time" that discursively obscure basics such as what work is actually being done where. For women in particular, IT work may be simply "time-shifted" to balance the demands of their unpaid work.

Additionally, expectations of employee "flexibility" can mean that IT workers are assumed to be available at all times, accessible by e-mail, cell phone, or pager. Their combined work time may actually expand rather than contract. The notion of "space" is a prevalent one in discussions of technological work. While work is often understood as being performed in "virtual spaces," the physical location of work is significant.

Professional, "high-tech" work tends to be located near large urban centers with an educated and diverse population, while low-status "outsourced" and "low-tech" work, such as call centers, may be more geographically dispersed and its flourishing may depend on higher unemployment in smaller urban and rural locales. However, even more high-end types of occupations, such as programmers, are being geographically dispersed to regions such as Southeast Asia and the Caribbean, where the cost of labour is lower. Geography is crucial for showing migration patterns and centers of high-tech and low-tech work.

On a smaller scale, IT has enabled work to be done from home, but at the same time, it has also dissolved many boundaries between home and work space. As with work time, work space flows into new domains, resulting in increased loads for women who already spend a great deal of time managing domestic labour. Research has clearly demonstrated a significant difference between male and female teleworkers. Men who telework in IT professions tend to be more affluent professionals who regard working at home as an upgrade in status and autonomy. Women who telework in IT professions tend to do it to manage childcare and other domestic demands, and they may work in low-status occupations such as data entry.

Fuzzy temporal-spatial language makes the extent of actual labour invisible while creating a fiction of a special alternative technological workspace. Thus it is critical to determine clearly what work is done where and when.

Indicators of Time and Place of Work:

1. Employment location
   a. Home
   b. Workplace
   c. Distance to employer
2. Geography
   a. Province, state, and/or region
   b. Census metropolitan area (CMA)
   c. Rural-urban area
3. Hours and schedule of work
   a. Average usual hours of work, paid and unpaid
   b. Work schedule: regular shifts, irregular shifts, etc.
4. Year
   a. Though concordances are available, occupational labels for many technological occupations did not officially exist before NAICS reclassification in 1997.

INDICATORS OF WORK CONTEXT AND ORGANIZATION

Many technical occupations are performed in so-called nontechnical industries. Similarly, technical industries can include nontechnical occupations. Thus, when trying to get a clear picture of the IT labour force, it is essential to look at both industry and occupation and, if possible, to combine them. A researcher might also look at how the work itself is organized in terms of technological changes to work. How and why were new technologies introduced, for example? In many female-dominated professions, new technologies have been introduced for the specific purpose of deskilling and eliminating women's jobs.

On the other hand, many IT-involved tasks, such as Web page design and network management, have been introduced into clerical work, and expectations for workers' technical skills have increased. A couple of major methodological problems exist in studying women's IT work. First, IT occupations emerge rapidly. Institutionalized occupational classifications do not emerge rapidly.

Thus, a researcher who wished to use data from Statistics Canada's Labour Force survey, for example, to see how many network architects were female in the 1990s would not have been able to, for these job categories did not exist prior to 2001. Second, women in particular are less likely to self-define as technical workers. In my interview data sample, women who worked in IT professions did not always define themselves as technical, regardless of what their job actually entailed. Nevertheless, in a limited context, industrial and occupational data can be useful in creating a broad demographic picture of the IT workforce.

Indicators of Work Context and Organization:

1. Industry
2. Occupation
3. Technological change
   a. What technological changes took place
   b. Purpose of technological change in workplace (according to employer)
   c. Experiences of technological change according to employee; for example, offered training in new technologies

INDICATORS OF WORK COMPENSATION

There is still a gendered pay gap in IT. Immigrant women of color working in IT fare worst of all, relative to white, Canadian-born men. This situation is hardly surprising to anyone who studies the labour market in general, but it is nevertheless ironic given the promises of IT as a new, meritocratic field.

Moreover, in the optimistic 1990s, IT was shaped by a venture capitalist ethos that rejected the wage protections of unions and attempted to substitute stock payoffs for consistent salaries and benefits. The presumed IT workforce was composed largely of young white men who rarely saw the need for provisions such as parental or disability leave. With the downturn in the IT sector throughout the late 1990s and early 2000s, wages and benefits are key issues for IT workers. IT women workers' commonly lower wages mean that women continue to be at a systemic disadvantage relative to male IT workers.

Indicators of Work Compensation:

1. Wages
   a. Hourly wage
   b. Annual earnings
   c. Income from combined sources (for example, stock options)
   d. Unpaid work, including nondomestic and caregiving work (for example, self-checkout, online banking)
2. "Social wage"
   a. Benefits
   b. Pension plan

INDICATORS OF THE LABOUR PROCESS

Simply put, what tasks are actually being done by IT workers? While IT work is often treated as a rather opaque category, within the industry not all tasks are equally valued. For example, although a non-IT person may not know the difference, technical support personnel are seen by IT workers as part of a lower occupational order than, say, systems engineers. What tasks are performed may only have a loose relationship to dimensions such as formal educational credentials. In addition, the complexity and skill demand of various tasks may not be reflected in work compensation.

Indicators of Labour Process:

1. Tasks performed
   a. In the home
   b. In the workplace
2. Technology used
   a. In the home
   b. In the workplace

In the previous section, I identified many points of entry and many dimensions that might be combined to map out the intersecting relations of IT work in greater depth. I do not mean to suggest that using several indicators of gendered IT work should result in a sort of relativism in which no structural relation is significant. The historical record of women's employment demonstrates that one of the most profound divisions of labour and work value is along the axis of gender, but other axes of differentiation are also critical.

A researcher who wishes to depict this diversity will thus encounter and recognize some tension here. On the one hand, IT work represents many new opportunities for women. On the other hand, persistent industrial and occupational segregation based on gender, race and ethnicity, immigrant status, age, geography, and other structural relations continues to shape women's work experiences in IT.

For example, one of the most popular occupations for women in IT is Web design. This occupation requires a breadth of skills, including graphic design, database development, and programming (though its skill requirements are increasing). It is also one of the lowest paid and most unstable occupations because it is often based on short-term work in which the worker is positioned as a "self-employed independent contractor," thus ineligible for statutory benefits. As jobs become female-typed, workers performing them are more likely to be paid less and to face limitations on their opportunities for advancement.

Though many women in IT are working hybrid jobs, hybridity does not increase the job's status; indeed, it may create new female job ghettos and employer expectations of expanded, "flexible" working time and space. Moreover, the multidimensional analysis I suggest must be set in a socioeconomic context of deepening employment precariousness and the erosion of stable employment relationships that affect both women and men, though somewhat differently.

What this brief introduction to a multidimensional analysis of the gendered organization of the IT workforce contributes to the debate is, first, the importance of an intersectional approach, an "analog continuum" rather than a "digital binary" construct for theorizing relations of gender and technology. Second, this writing contributes a call to situate such intersections within the material conditions of shifts in employment patterns, including increasing employment instability in tandem with an erosion of statutory protections and regulation. This chapter calls for an examination of what work is actually being done, by whom, and how, and what role the technologies and structural social relations play.

A multidisciplinary analysis, using various types of data collection, is an ideal approach. For example, I was alerted to the issue of occupational hybridity through my interview subjects. I would not have discovered and isolated it had I restricted my investigation to statistical labour force data alone. Indeed, the real work of the interview subjects would have remained invisible. Third, this piece contributes methodological guidelines for studying work in IT, which, while they draw on the well-developed literature on women in scientific and "hard technology" fields, nevertheless represent a slight departure from studies about women in those broader fields, because of the occupational hybridity that characterizes the IT field.

Identifying persistently gendered employment trends and work (de)valuation need not result in oversimplification. This approach attempts to reflect the diversity of technology as social practice, the power relations inherent in the organization and experience of that work, and the significance of global labour-market trends in helping us understand why and how work is evolving as it is. It is critical for us to move beyond simple dichotomous analyses of "male-female" and "technical-nontechnical" to create a rich, nuanced picture of gendered IT work in the twenty-first century.

EMPOWERING WOMEN AND TECHNOLOGY

In 1998, we wrote a grant to support our desires for educational change at our university. Our teaching experiences indicated that women, especially women of color, arrive at our working-class urban university lacking basic computer skills, that is, knowledge about how to use a computer and how to run basic word-processing, Web browsing, and e-mail programs. Laurie Fuller's introductory Web-enhanced women's studies courses often enrolled first-generation women university students, fresh from the urban public school system, with limited knowledge of the use of computers.

Erica Meiners' graduate educational theory classes consisted of returning adult students, predominantly women, who entered the university after years outside educational contexts; in addition to anxiety about returning to school, they worried about all the "new" technological skills that courses assumed they possessed. Fueled by this problem in our everyday context and feeling energetic after participating in a grant-writing seminar at our university, we started research for a proposal to access resources to intervene.

Researching and writing this proposal shifted us, as feminist academics and organizers, from our relatively familiar epistemological terrain populated by antiracist feminist theories and praxes and by queer theories and communities to a landscape inhabited by frameworks of liberal multiculturalism, positivism, and a "politically and ideologically neutral" language of educational reform. We quickly found that literature in the area of the problem of women and minorities in the science pipeline frequently signified what we observed at our institution: women continue to be underrepresented in technology, especially in professions that require computer expertise.

In science, math, engineering, and technology (SMET), women learn better in a single-sex environment and where relationships are involved, as in cooperative-learning groups. Additionally, research frames the absence of people of color, white women, or both in SMET as an economic problem for the nation-state. We used this discussion of the potential negative consequences for "our" U.S. economic (and military) dominance in our proposal as funding sources often state that based on this rationale, they would fund research to identify strategies to recruit and retain women and minorities in SMET fields.

Our library check-out lists shifted from cyberfeminist theories and works by transnational antiracist feminist theorists that question the inherent "good" of technology to government-funded reports, research studies, and texts that used frameworks to construct technology as inherently "good" or "neutral." Based on the language of the official request for proposals (RFP) of the granting agency we targeted, it was clear that successful proposals originated from a positivistic and a (mythic. politically neutral epistemological terrain.

We acquired a vocabulary that worked with this paradigm (empowerment, lifelong learning, assessment and evaluation, curricular transformation, quantitative data gathering) and jettisoned familiar terms that signified discourses of poststructuralism, feminism, or critical (race) theory, and we eliminated language that could be perceived as postmodern (dialogues, discussions of power imbalances between students or subjects and professor or principal investigator, reciprocity) or political (feminist, white supremacy). This desire to pass with a "neutral ideology" also influenced our visions of educational change, as the RFP clearly stated that projects could not discriminate against anyone. (Note, of course, that this requirement for nondiscrimination comes from the critical work of earlier paradigm changers).

Our visions of a (feminist) "women only" project could not be explicitly named or advertised as for "women only," even though the purpose of our study and intervention was to create a single-sex classroom environment for women. We wrote and animated this neutral paradigm despite our belief that race- and gender-neutral educational change is not feasible, and despite knowing that research has demonstrated "neutrality" is not effective. Margaret Eisenhardt and Elizabeth Finkel found that race- and gender-neutral environments in the sciences are neutral only to the white males who construct that environment.

In addition, our varied political work has led us to view "race neutral" as frequently a code word for supporting white supremacy. Minorities, a term that we would not use in our teaching, academic, or activist writing, immediately became an issue. Our preference, given the connotations of the term minorities-less than (whites) in importance and also less than (whites) in numbers-was people of color or women of color, yet the call for proposals (and most of the research data. used the term minorities. (Significantly, the data on the problem of women and minorities in the science pipeline is often represented in ways that separate "women" and "people of color" into two discrete groups.)

We did not know if this critique of and sensitivity to the term empower was shared by government funding agencies; therefore we chose to use empower and minorities. We spent months working on this proposal to increase the technological literacy levels of women at an urban working-class university in the Midwest. We did not include our ideas about dismantling (or even questioning the neutrality or the assumed inherent good of) the nation-state or educating women to resist white-supremacist capitalist patriarchy but instead wrote a request for money to help "women and minorities" join in the economy.

Fortuitously, the American Association of University Women (AAUW) published a report stating "technology was the new boys' club," and we hooked our grant proposal onto their research findings. We wrote fifteen pages articulating a seamless vision of a (closeted feminist) intervention that we believed would facilitate institutional change. What are the consequences of writing in this different genre to access institutional resources? Professionals use a variety of social languages many times in one day. Why should the use of terms such as minorities or empower constrain us?

Language is not neutral; language shapes ways of thinking about ourselves and the world we inhabit. Using the granting agency's language validates an epistemological framework of multiculturalism that is, at best, problematic, and this has the capacity literally to produce subjects and create realities. Our original feminist praxis-project, born out of the desire to intervene in a local problem, had morphed to require us to defend language and paradigms we previously critiqued, to promise replicable products (when we did not think curriculum was portable or worked when decontextualized), to prepare and promote workforce development for the nation-state, to advocate "race- and gender-neutral" educational change, and to advertise Lifelong Success through Computer Expertise.

We envisioned the grant with social change as the goal, not the increase and diversification of the labour market; yet to get the money; and performed the latter. Our idea was an immature "take the money and run" strategy in which female students would get the skills to enter the labour market and support themselves, and simultaneously they would resist white supremacist capitalist patriarchy. Our project, "Empowering Women for Life-Long Success through Computer Expertise," was funded for four years.

The proposal focused on creating a course that would give women at our institution the tools to succeed at using technology. Four years later, when we reviewed the data collected and reflected on the project, we recognized that the single-sex course held no interest to students at our institution. Instead, the most useful to the participants, and the most surprising to us, was the creation of a small lab and the employment of students to staff the lab and tutor other students.

Given the research on women's successes learning technology in single-sex environments, coupled with background and familiarity in women's studies environments, we had not thought (nor did the literature on single-sex education) that the single-sex aspect of the course would be a deterrent. The brochure we developed to advertise the course had photos of women, used the language-"specifically designed for women" and "targeted for women"-and cited data about the state's need for technology workers.

Interviews with women who enrolled in the women-only sections demonstrated that they had selected this class not because it was women only-but because of the technology and the statistics cited on the brochure in relation to job opportunities. Interviews further illustrated that many of the female students in fact thought about not taking the class, and they had to defend to family and friends their reasons for taking a course for women only.

This presented a problem throughout the project and illustrates how heteronormativity affects women's educational trajectories. In addition, this wrinkle caused us to reframe our visions of curricular feminist change. Low enrollment does not mean that students would not benefit from participating in the course; yet women at our institution expressed reluctance to take a women-only course. If no female students enroll, despite creative marketing strategies, the course is not an effective educational intervention, nor is it the "best" environment. In addition, little of the literature that looks at the efficacy of women-only learning environments adequately addresses the ways race and class affect single-sex learning environments.

The multi-racial, working-class population that attends our university calls into question single-sex learning environments that do not take into account race and class. Our proposal suggested that curricular transformation would be the location of change; however, empowerment came not from curricular transformation but from peer tutoring and informal workshops. This unanticipated result highlighted the importance of creating spaces where students can participate as legitimate university community members (for our population, this means in part as paid workers) and learn without the notable presence of a teacher, a class or curriculum.

The grant funded a computer lab with five machines, a telephone, a printer, and peer mentors and lab assistants to assist and teach students technology. The lab is located next to the women's studies office, and sofas and coffee tables furnish a small common area outside the lab. Three Latinas and one returning adult white woman composed the first group of assistants, hired in 2000. They decorated the lab with feminist and justice posters and labeled all the computers with the names of famous women scientists. They used the lab as a site for their own work, socializing, and organizing (usually after working hours).

Their job was to staff the lab and teach other students-help them learn to e-mail, to use spreadsheets, to create Web pages, and so forth. They placed signs across the campus and made business cards that they delivered to classes (first to women's studies classes and faculty and then expanding to others) to let students (and faculty) know that one-on-one help was available. Fifteen women have worked part-time as lab assistants over the past four years: five Latinas, one African American, two Asian Americans, one white woman in her early 50s, one recent immigrant from Eastern Europe, and five whites.

The assistants work with a range of technological and often academic problems and a variety of students (from women's studies, psychology, education, business, and other departments): the eighty-year-old woman who audits courses and immediately forgets what she learned at the last tutoring session; students who are recent immigrants and left villages with no electricity; students who have no computer at home, did not use a computer in their high school classes, and need help learning the skills to complete a specific assignment.

The assistants' jobs require that they practice the technological skills they acquire, and they become innovative technological and academic troubleshooters. From observation and interviews, it is clear that lab assistants learned from teaching: they increased their own skill levels, became better able to navigate the university and academic context, improved their writing skills, and increased their confidence levels. Most of the lab assistants are first-generation university students who support themselves (and often their families) with loans, scholarships, and part-time employment-representative of the larger undergraduate population at our university.

Typically, the part-time employment these lab assistants had prior to working in our lab consisted of low-wage service industry jobs. Rose, a twenty-two-year-old Latina, worked as a telemarketer and as a fast-food cashier; while this labour enabled her to support herself and her daughter (with some assistance from her family), the jobs did not enhance her resume, nor did they support or coincide with her academic and professional goals (to work in law enforcement). The paid employment that women did before working in the lab (waitperson, telemarketer, service sales representative, child-care worker, and fast-food cashier) was feminized nonunion service-sector work.

At the lab, the assistants were the experts, they had knowledge and skills that others wanted, and they worked in these "expertise" positions in cross-generational and cross-racial contexts. They spoke of feeling empowered by their skills and their success. They referred to their work as "teaching" or "working in the lab," and this gave them a meaningful campus and employment identity. The material contexts these women face in their lives, how to support themselves and/or their families on low wages, is a critical factor that shapes their academic trajectory.

When roles as "worker" and "student" conflict, as is the case for many of our students who swell the ranks of the low-wage service-industry sector, the material realities-paying rent, supplying food, and even covering tuition-surpass paying attention in classes. The lab assistants managed to avoid some of this role conflict. They worked in the same physical spaces in which they studied, and their identity as "worker" overlapped with their identity as "student."

The lab also became a site for feminist, queer, and other student organizing. In 2001-2002 a lab assistant was also the organizer of the Gay Lesbian Bisexual Alliance (GLBA) on campus, and another was the organizer of the Feminist Majority Leadership Alliance (FMLA). These student clubs used the lab to create promotional materials for events, to communicate electronically with members of the group, and to do research projects together. The lab space was routinely full of books, posters, notes about campus and community events, pamphlets, and lab participants (or assistants) homework.

Learning or legitimate peripheral participation in communities of practice "is a process that takes place in a participation framework, not in an individual mind." Thus, learning happens in communities. There was no formal curriculum, no teacher, and no classroom structure, yet the lab assistants, their peers, and the social communities they were a part of learned technology. The two student groups (FMLA and GLBA) used technology as a tool to organize and create relationships. Students wanted to work together to make Web pages for the FMLA or the GLBA; they used technology as a tool for community building and advancing social and political practices they were invested in.

As the project concludes, we consider not merely the data we have compiled from this research initiative and the intervention we staged but the more discrete components of the project. What are the consequences of a "take the money and run" strategy for those committed to progressive (often radical) social reform in and outside the academy? How does participation in mainstream discursive and epistemological paradigms shift and constrain us in politically untenable positions? How can we access the resources to fuel progressive social change yet resist the recuperative power of dominant, multifaceted institutions and discourses?

Engagement with this project exemplifies a "women's studies" dilemma; how to work within a system one is trying to change. Women's studies scholarship and activism encounter these tensions in the academy and beyond, and the theme of feminist change erupts as we reflect on the project. What subversions are possible, given Audre Lorde's statement about power? "The master's tools will never dismantle the master's house. They may allow us temporarily to beat him at his own game, but they will never enable us to bring about genuine change" (emphasis added).

The feminist geographer and activist Ruth Gilmore, writing against the mass incarceration movement, also argues against static notions of power and resistance (working from the writings of Audre Lorde): "One works with what is at hand; the problem is not the 'master's tools' but the effective control of those 'tools.'" While Gilmore's caution is important, and one of our "tools," language, is clearly not inherently oppressive, contexts can and do control and affix meanings to language that limit, for example, justice initiatives.

Yet, in the messy work of praxis, perhaps tools can be temporarily re-formed or a different use for the old tools can be forged? Empowering minority women can be a success story of technological skills acquisition and agency and simultaneously a tale of the reproduction of (low-wage) technology workers for the nation-state. Perhaps this doubled move is a kind of tactical resistance? Or, this is the story we tell ourselves at the end of the day. Our advice to (sister) activists is-proceed with caution. There is no neat and happy ending. Our project, "Empowering Women for Life-Long Success through Computer Expertise," did enable female students who completed the course to attain a higher level of confidence and technological abilities.

The meaningful (and paid) apprenticeship of the lab assistants during the same period enabled them to acquire a wider range of skills and, most important, a kind of technological fluency. Although acquiring the resources to support this change was significant, negotiating how language and epistemological frameworks shape and constrain projects and political action also has been a valuable "finding." We end the project with the knowledge that we were naive to hope to "take the money and run," yet the process enabled us to gain perspective on the importance of implementing (and theorizing) educational and institutional change.

8

The Digital Revolution

Literacy as a source of empowerment has shifted from the print to the computer medium. There is the lingering danger that cyberspace will solidify the gap between the haves and the have-nots. However, this gap cannot merely be reduced to economic difference and financial access to Internet technology. Certainly, what appear to be cultural reasons for the digital divide are often due to differences in economic opportunity.

But while it is difficult to distinguish whether economic or cultural factors are more salient in explaining the digital divide, the different levels of interaction between religious traditions and technological changes raise several crucial questions: how will a computer revolution shape the changes within religious doctrine, and how do religious traditions affect people's ability to adapt to such a revolution? Examining how technology has affected doctrine and gender in Islam will illuminate a key example of the interplay between technology and religion.

By exploring the effect of the Internet on the internal logic of Islam, as well as the enlarged global influence Islam must play when digital barriers are broken, we hope to highlight the possibilities for a dual reformation.

INFORMATION TO REFORMATION

The impact of the first industrial revolution on western Christianity undoubtedly led to the momentous movement of the Christian Reformation. Will the impact of the new revolution of information lead to a comparable Islamic Reformation? In the 20th century Westerners have debated whether the Protestant Reformation was the mother of capitalism in Europe or whether the Christian Reformation was itself a child of earlier phases of the capitalist revolution. Max Weber's book The Protestant Ethic and the Spirit of Capitalism advances the view that the Protestant Reformation was the mother of capitalism rather than a child of economic change. Other thinkers, however, have identified pre-Reformation technological inventions as part of the preparation for both the birth of Protestantism and modern-day capitalism.

Francis Robinson, professor of history at the University of London, has placed the printing press at the center of the Protestant movement and within the Catholic counter-offensive. He writes, "Print lay at the heart of that great challenge to religious authority, the Protestant Reformation; Lutheranism was the child of the printed book. Print lay at the heart of the Catholic counter-offensive, whether it meant harnessing the press for the work of Jesuits and the office of Propaganda, or controlling the press through the machinery of the Papal Index and the Papal Imprimatur." The question here is whether the Internet and cyberspace and the third industrial revolution will do to Islam what the first industrial revolution did for Christianity.

In some respects the Christian Reformation was a return to the biblical roots of Christianity. Likewise, the information revolution may help Islam realize some of its earliest aims more effectively. The first casualty of the information revolution, however, may be national sovereignty, which will shrink in the wake of the Internet and cyberspace. The printed word played a major role in the construction of nation hood and in reinforcing national consciousness. Computer communication, on the other hand, is contributing to the breakdown of nationhood and may play a role in the construction of trans-ethnic communities.

While the first industrial revolution of capitalist production and the Christian reformation became allied to the new forces of nationalism in the Western world, the third industrial revolution and any Islamic reformation will be increasingly hostile to the insularity of the state. Islam and the information revolution will be allies in breaking down the barriers of competing national sovereignties. The new technology will give Islam a chance to realize its original aim of transnational universalism. The Internet could become the Islamic super-highway.

Many Muslims have already risen to this challenge of the new information age with Islamic resource guides on the Internet, Cyber Muslim Guides, the Islamic Information and News Network, and web servers with Islamic material. As Childers writes, contrary to some assumptions that "modem communications would engender a new and generally Western-oriented cosmopolitanism, they are predominantly spreading the idea of a freedom that is translated by the receivers as endogenous freedom- including freedom to rejoin one's real kinship (whether larger or smaller) and to re-examine the validity of one's own ancient social values." Thus, the Internet may have the effect of rekindling community.

THE BALLOT ENTERS THE HAREM

But there is one fundamental area where Islam and the new information revolution have yet to converge: the relationship between men and women. Will the new information technology fundamentally alter gender relations? The Muslim world has traditionally vacillated between two doctrines on this issue. One doctrine has been to treat genders as separate but equal. Genders co-exist in homes; separation of genders is inevitably moderated by family ties. This is qualitatively different from the separation of races and ethnicities. The gender doctrine of "separate but equal" could survive the new information revolution.

Under the new technology the computerized hijab is at hand: women can more easily stay at home while continuing to participate in a computerized workplace. This possibility is amply demonstrated by a woman from the British Asian community in her response to a BBC radio presenter who expressed concern that the computer can, in fact, enhance the isolation of women. The woman commented, "Well, if they're just stuck at home then why not use the Internet to get connectivity with people across the world... the Internet can also provide an access for women to possibly start providing their own services maybe hobbies that they're interested in or business that they have a keen eye on."

By gradually abolishing the distinction between home and the workplace, Internet technology may give women the opportunity to integrate themselves into the economic and political global community. But many Muslim societies treat women as "separate and unequal." Aspects of that perspective are rooted in a view of the Shari'a that dictates that women inherit half of what men inherit and that, in certain circumstances, holds the testimony of women in court to be worth less than that of men. Such Muslim societies have assumed that there were two different doors of knowledge, one for each gender. Many Muslim societies had assumed that there were branches of knowledge that were not fit for women and children under 16. The Taliban regime in Afghanistan has carried this theory of two tiers of gender knowledge to its extreme.

New information technology is going to destroy the social justification for gender discrimination. Increased information may be insusceptible to gender differentiation. The digital divide may give way to digital democracy. While it is true that what men know about sex, pornography, politics, and corruption may also be accessible to women through the Internet, the new technology will pass a death sentence on the old tradition of female seclusion that has existed since the Abbasid dynasty in many Muslim societies. The traditional forms of seclusion of women will no longer survive a technology in which women can declare their presence and, in time, assert their rights.

TOWARD ISLAMIZING THE INTERNET

In spite of these new freedoms and new possibilities afforded by the Internet, the technology is not necessarily free of influence from existing systems of economic, political, and social inequality. New computer technology and the Internet may be inaugurating new kinds of stratification and reform, and Muslim countries are bound to be affected. Distribution of real power in the world is not based on "who owns what" but on "who knows what." It has not been the power of property but the power of skill that has been the ultimate international arbiter.

For example, oil-rich Muslim countries like Saudi Arabia or Kuwait have not been able to exploit their own petroleum resources without the skills of Western companies and their engineers. How is the Muslim ummab to relate to these "negative" consequences of the Internet and computer communication? There is now a growing movement among Muslims that seeks to Islamize scientific (and other forms) of knowledge for the greater project of Islamizing modernity itself. The Islamization of computer communication is seen as a core component of this quest.

As Nasim Butt explains, "As information technologies are becoming the basic tools of manipulation and control, access to them will become the decisive factor between control and power or manipulation and subservience. In this powerful dilemma, the way forward, surely, is to modify the technology at the point of use to meet the needs and requirements of Muslim society." Butt suggests an alternative scientific paradigm that supposedly maintains the values of Islam and provides some broad guidelines for the Islamization of science and technology.

Science in the more isolationist Muslim discourse has often been viewed as distinct from religion. More recent Islamic revival initiatives, however, insist on a greater convergence between the two. There is a new nostalgia for ancient scientific practices. Advocates seek to enforce Islamic ethical parameters on both scientific research and, more importantly, on applied science. Some Islamicist interpretations would now regard any scientific venture that carries the potential for harmful or unnatural consequences as un-Islamic.

Under this paradigm, research into germ warfare would probably be disallowed outright. But how about areas of mixed blessings, like genetic engineering, which may have beneficial or unnatural and harmful uses? The verdict here may depend on the particular application. For example, nuclear weapons have been seen as defensive against Zionist, Hindu, or Western enemies. Pakistan's development of a nuclear weapons program may be a rationalization of this interpretation.

The Islamization of science may also refer to attempts to accord science greater Islamic identity and Muslim representation. At some point this quest may entail both indigenization and domestication. Indigenization involves increasing the use of indigenous resources, ranging from native personnel to aspects of traditional local knowledge, in the process making them more relevant to the modern age. Domestication, on the other hand, involves making imported versions of science and technology more relevant to local needs.

In the realm of computer technology, domestication would begin with a substantial employment of indigenous personnel. This would require, first, greater commitment by Muslim governments and institutions to promote relevant training at different levels for Muslims, both men and women; second, readiness on the part of both governments and employers to create a structure of incentives that would attract Muslim men and women to those fields; third, greater political pressure on computer suppliers to facilitate training and cooperate in related tasks; and fourth, stricter control by Muslim governments of the importation of computers.

The indigenization of high-level personnel in the local computer industry should in time help indigenize the functions of computer technology. When the most skilled roles in the computer industry in a Muslim country are in the hands of Muslims themselves, new types of technological tasks will emerge. This Islamization of computer personnel should also facilitate further Islamization of users of computer services. But efficient indigenization and domestication of the computer still require a gradualist and planned approach.

The difficulty of this task is compounded by the technological dependence engendered by multinational corporations and their respective governments. As technology levels increase in Muslim countries, so too may these counties' dependence on external corporations in order to maintain the technology. Additional strategies for decolonization of computer technology are thus required. These may include diversification of the sources on which a county is dependent, horizontal interpenetration to promote greater exchange between Muslim countries themselves, and vertical counterpenetration to enable Muslim countries to work in the citadels of power in the West.

LAUNCHING ISLAM

The possibility that the Internet may stimulate an "Islamic Reformation" is based on the assumption that individual Muslim men and women are real actors in the information revolution and not merely objects, and that they are producers of knowledge and not merely consumers of knowledge. Are Muslims of both genders making progress in narrowing the technological gap between Islam and the West?

But what would be the larger global implications of an Islamic Reformation? Will not a reinvigorated Muslim ummab lead to the clash of civilizations, as predicted by Harvard professor Samuel Huntington? It can be argued that Islamic renewal will not only galvanize the Muslim ummab from within but also, by rekindling the spirit of ijtihad, it will reopen the doors of constructive engagement with other civilizations.

At the height of its glory Islam attempted to protect religious minorities, even if Muslims did not always respect women's rights. Jews and Christians had special status as People of the Book, a fraternity of monotheists. Other religious minorities were later to be accorded the status of dhimmis (protected minorities). Under the system Jewish scholars rose to high positions in Muslim Spain.

During the Ottoman Empire, Christians also sometimes attained high political office: Sulaiman I (1520-1566) had Christian ministers in his government, as did Salim III (1789-1807). The Mughal Empire integrated Hindus and Muslims into a consolidated Indian state; Emperor Akbar (1556-1605) carried furthest the Mughal policy of bringing Hindus into the government. All this may be an indication that Islam is inclusive and open to dialogue precisely when it is politically most influential. It is this historical precedent that is likely to undergo resurgence under an Islamic Reformation. A self-confident and self-assured Islam is a better partner for peace than a threatened Islam.

The toughest synthesis of all is yet to come - synthesizing the rights of women with the rights of men to create a more balanced moral equilibrium. It would be particularly fitting if the Martin Luther of the Islamic Reformation turned out to be a woman, posting her 95 theses of refonn not on the door of a Wittenberg mosque but universally on the Internet.

DIGITAL TECHNOLOGIES AND PEDAGOGIES

New digital technologies and multimedia are transforming how we teach and learn. They are transforming our classrooms from spaces of delivery to spaces of active inquiry and authorship. New digital media are empowering students to become researchers, storytellers, historians, oral historians, and cultural theorists in their own right. Whether constructing their own life stories or interpreting the life stories of others, the digital format transforms students' capacity to synthesize, interpret, theorize, and create new cultural and historical knowledge. In this way, digital formats potentially democratize learning and produce critical subjects and authors.

The four short essays that follow are snapshots of experiments with new media in our respective classrooms. They were presented at the Annual Meeting of the Oral History Association, in San Diego, California, to a standing-room only audience. Tracey Weis' African American History students conduct archival research in Web-based historic sites and repositories, and construct collaborative interpretations in PowerPoint. Through their digital presentations, students become more conscious of, and reflective about, the power and responsibilities of historical synthesis and interpretation.

Rina Benmayor incorporates Digital Storytelling in her Latina Life Stories class. Students, the majority of whom are

Latina/o, author their own life stories digitally, combining voice, music, and images. Then, they theorize their digital stories, much the way Latina writers have done, exploring how to create new knowledge and theory. Cecilia O'Leary's students construct Digital Histories, many of which are family oral histories. The digital storytelling form authorizes them to lay claim to their own histories, their own voice, and to use primary sources in authoritative ways. Digital history-telling enables students to see themselves as citizen-historians.

Bret Eynon works with a predominantly immigrant student body of color. His students conduct oral histories with their peers and develop electronic portfolios, in which hypertext facilitates multifaceted self-representation. The four of us are principal researchers in the Visible Knowledge Project (VKP). Headquartered at Georgetown University, VKP is a five-year, multi-million-dollar project involving 70 faculty and 21 college and university campuses nationwide. It is one of the most significant projects in technology and learning, and the largest in the humanities, social sciences, and interdisciplinary culture fields.

Through its focus on student learning and faculty development in technology-enhanced environments, faculty investigators are exploring effective pedagogies that incorporate new media technologies. Research projects focus on creating and researching models of teaching and learning that promote distributive learning, authentic tasks, complex inquiry, dialogic learning, constructive learning, public accountability, reflection, and critical thinking. Within VKP, the four of us comprise a Digital Storytelling Affinity Group. Through videoconferencing, we share our work with each other and with other faculty across the country; we discuss pedagogical strategies and tools, give workshops and conference presentations, and co-author articles such as this one.

In retrospect, however, this relatively recent innovation in my teaching had its origins in my experiences as a community organizer in the central Appalachian coalfields 20 years ago. Living in communities characterized by large-scale absentee ownership, environmental degradation, and increasing levels of poverty, coalfield residents imaginatively used images of various kinds (posters, photographs, and slide shows) to tell stories of their lives and communities that contradicted "official" versions of events.

Accessible and relatively inexpensive media permitted residents in strip-mining areas (and in gentrifying urban cores) to exchange sets of slides that documented the challenges they faced and the strategies and forms of resist ance they employed. Similarly, deploying new media in college classrooms enables students to tell stories of their own lives and communities in ways that allow them to gain an authoritative claim on the past.

A comparative focus on historic places, as "tangible forms of. our legacy from preceding generations that embody and reflect the traditions, experiences, ideas, and controversies of our past," connects these ostensibly local and national investigations. In this course, we consider nationally known historic sites as essentially local sites that are deeply embedded in community and regional economic, political, social, and cultural contexts. Students conduct a virtual field study at the beginning of the semester to identify and evaluate the practical and theoretical advantages of using historic sites (or places) as "laboratories" for learning history.

Working in teams, they combine their observations as virtual visitors to selected historic sites with add itional research to produce and present PowerPoint presentations, complete with narration. The implicit objective of this exercise is to encourage students to compare and contrast the content and tone of interpretations presented by public historians in historical sites and academic historians in scholarly journals. This inquiry, then, invites students to situate themselves as participants in the ongoing debate about the significance of race and slavery in American history and culture.

The exercise began with paired online exploration of four historic sites that interpret the colonial and early national periods: Monticello, Mount Vernon, Colonial Williamsburg, and the National Park Service. To complicate the reading of the original Web sites (and to forestall conventional responses such as "no one questioned slavery in this time period," "everyone accepted it," or "the Founding Fathers had no choice"), each group was asked to examine a second Web site that presented an alternative or contradictory narrative of race and slavery.

For example, the Mount Vernon group examined an online biography of Ona Judge Staines, a bondswoman who escaped from George and Martha Washington in June 1796 while the Washingtons were in residence in Philadelphia. Consulting *America: History and Life*, an online periodical index, these students found pertinent information that they could use to support both George Washington's defense and Ona Judge Staines' accusations for their presentation, "Mt. Vernon:

A Slave's Haven? Or Hell?" George Washington defended himself against charges of harsh and cruel treatment by pointing out that enslaved men and women on other plantations endured worse living and working conditions. Ona Judge's allegations were bolstered by observations made by visitors to Mt. Vernon, among them Henrietta Liston, the wife of the British ambassador. "Everyone knows George Washington," the students acknowledged at the beginning of their presentation, "but what about Ona [Judge Staines]?"

Ona Judge Staines' courage in fleeing slavery and her refusal, despite repeated entreaties from the Washingtons, to return to Mount Vernon, raised vexing questions about "good" masters and encouraged students to rethink benevolent paternalism. So, how do digital tools affect the act and process of telling the story? Using digital tools shapes how novice historians approach the fundamental challenge of establishing temporal order, how to assemble what frequently seems to them to be discrete and unrelated fragments into coherent narratives.

For example, something inspired or enabled one team of students telling the story of Colonial Williamsburg to situate its story in the broader context of the evolution of slavery in Virginia and in colonial America. The imperative of a multimedia format forces a greater rigor in deciding what to show and what to tell. The redundancy, for example, of merely reading the slide is obvious-if not to the storytellers in the preparation stage, then to the storytellers and the audience in the actual presentation.

In their efforts to avoid boring repetition, students are challenged to elaborate a point of view and to develop a perspective about what they are showing. Although students can struggle to fill a slide in the s ame way they agonize to fill a page, it seems that novice historians can more easily "see" the difference between presenting evidence of various kinds (showing) and explaining the significance of the evidence (telling).

Do digital stories tell or reveal in ways that conventional historical essays do not? Less likely simply to report as they do in their papers, novices working with multimedia are more confident and more tentative. They are more convinced that their research has complicated, rather than resolved, the vexing questions posed by the Websites of the various historic places. The effect has been to arouse, rather than dampen, intellectual curiosity and to make them more comfortable with assuming a more critical (even if at times a more provisional) stance.

They are more inclined to admit uncertainty and lack of resolution, and more inclined to come up with questions rather than definitive answers. In short, researching and retelling these stories about race and slavery persuaded most of these young historians that "reading historical sources directly allows [them] to make their own decisions about the meaning of the past and the intentions of historical characters".

In searching the Websites of various historic sites for the agency and presence of African Americans, the novice historians discovered their own narrative authority and historical sensibility. As they pondered how the authors of the Web site constructed their relations with their audiences and how the authors constituted themselves as authoritative interpreters of the past, they began to ask themselves fundamental questions about the purpose of history and memory making:

- What constitutes history?
- How is historical memory cultivated, perpetuated, deflected, and overturned?
- What do we need to know about the past and who is entitled to reconstruct it?
- How does the past help us make sense of the present?
- Who has the authority to answer these questions?

Approaching these historic sites as visitors and students of history, students in African American History moved from "outside the circle of cultural arbiters" to the inside circle of historic interpreters. They gained their own claims on the past by interrogating the controversies that these "tangible legacies" embodied and by telling more complicated stories of race and slavery than those presented at the sites.

"What is a digital story?" you are asking. Essentially, it is a three to four minute digital multimedia "movie" that combines an original story or script with images, music, and above all, a narration in the author's own voice. We are using this format to tell identity stories and to "theorize" them. We start by turning a personal narrative into a short script (about a page and one-half, double spaced). The author then records her/his script, selects and scans visuals (photographs, video, and creative drawings or clip art), and chooses a music track to run underneath.

For example, Jacinto's story is a tribute to his grandfather, to the many life lessons his grandfather taught him-above all, how to sing with all his heart and soul. Using the conventions of Chicano humor, Viana tells about "The Day I Became a Chicana," about awakening one morning to suddenly find her transformed, with an entirely new consciousness. Dawn reclaims her Bolivian identity and heritage, and denounces ways in which she is stereotyped and homogenized by mainstream society. Leon tells about his journey to re-center himself in his indigenous heritage.

Carlos reflects on his migration trajectory from rural Mexico to picking strawberrie s in California, to ESL classes, to community college, and finally, to the university. Emily, whose half sister and brother are mixed race, challenges identity based on color rather than on consciousness. Mary resists being forced to only check one identity box and claims her multiple identities and positionalities. Gabriela and Rocio name the cultural oppressions inscribed upon their bodies.

These stories are not born out of the blue. They are inspired by the autobiographical writings of Latinas and by the cultural theories these writings embody-the concepts of borderlands and new mestiza consciousness, hybrid identities that go beyond ethnic heritage, border feminism, and feminist latinidades. The readings trigger memories and emotions. Students, female and male, begin to voice their own stories in class-remembrances of painful, difficult, or joyful moments in their lives. For many, this is the first time they have thought about their lives as embodying larger social forces, theories, and identities.

Others find that the class unleashes long-held feelings. It provides a context for telling their stories and for drawing upon new theoretical thinking regarding identity, ethnicity, and culture. Students frequently find that they are now telling the story differently, putting it through historical and theoretical lenses they did not have before. Personal experience becomes theorized, situated. In the class, students also see the digital stories produced by previous classes.

Suddenly, they feel authorized to inscribe their voices and create their own digital texts. They begin to envision their own digital contributions to the testimonial literature on cultural identity. Many students find that in constructing this digital story, they are reconstructing a self, resituating their subjectivity within broader social frameworks. The stories link their tellers to real ?..d imagined communities of meaning and belonging. The digital medium also enables students to produce and "publish" their stories for multiple audiences of viewers and listeners.

Digital stories navigate through the Internet, through CD-ROMs, through public presentations, in family viewings, and become part of the broader corpus of Latina or life-story collections. The medium becomes a tool for constructing a self, but also for contributing new generational perspectives on identity, community, belonging, and selfhood. There is no gatekeeper here, no editorial competition, only encouragement to author life stories. In terms of production, the digital story is a more democratic form that enables new voices to emerge through an immediate and self-determined process. Creating the digital story has proved to be an empowering and transformative process.

These stories, which are by no means exceptional, were gathered by LaGuardia students, as part of a course that helps students see the college and their own lives as a part of major historical changes. "Going Places! Immigration, Education & Change in New York City, 1900-2002" is my version of a Liberal Arts capstone course. In this course, students examine the immigrant experience, past and present, using scholarly articles, films, novels, and Web sites. Their final project is an extended life history interview with another LaGuardia student, plus a 10-page paper that examines the links between that student's life and the themes and patterns studied in the course.

What different experiences do immigrant students have at LaGuardia? How do we as individuals experience and shape the individual, social, cultural, and political changes now framing the 21st century? What do students bring to the college from their families, their work, and their worlds? How does the process of going to college affect their families and their communities their own identities? These questions guide the project.

The project helps students examine their own experiences and place them in a larger social and historical context. It is a challenging research assignment, requiring students to conduct primary research and integrate their findings with insights from a range of sources. In the process, the students create a rich archive of first-person testimony, documenting and preserving a process of historical transformation.

LaGuardia is in one sense the equivalent of the Henry Street Settlement House, one of the famous institutions of 100 years ago, a border zone between the immigrant world and the dominant culture, a place where differences were negotiated and new cultures created. Historians would be delighted to find a cache of interviews documenting immigrant views of life in the settlement houses.

The students of Going Places are helping to document the complex life of a comparable contemporary institution, the experiences of its members, and, through them, the changes taking place in surrounding communities. What is particularly significant is that the students, the immigrants, are the ones asking the questions and writing the interpretations. Certain themes come up repeatedly in the student papers-and in the reflections of the student interviewers as well.

Over and over, students talk about how important education is to them, a route away from the dead-end jobs in restaurants and sweatshops that loom as alternatives. The mix of hope and desperation articulated by interviewers and interviewees is striking. Another common theme of the conversation is the powerful transformation of gender roles taking place in immigrant families and communities, a process fed by cultural and economic factors, as well as by educational processes; a recurring topic for female and male students is the excitement and uncertainty associated with this process. A third common theme is the way in which immigrant students struggle with their identity as Americans. Attracted by America and much that it stands for, LaGuardia's immigrant students are nonetheless ambivalent.

Digital technology plays a significant but not fundamental role in the "Going Places" classroom. Students examine web sites to learn more about immigration, historical and contemporary. They extensively use the discussion board on the course web site, sharing questions, problems, and ideas. The discussion board also facilitates the exchange of draft papers for peer editing processes, which students rate as one of the most valuable elements of the course. The site also provides a place where students deposit their final projects, creating a digital archive where student papers are available to scholars and other students.

In the future, digital tools will play an even larger role in this process. By 2004, students' Going Places projects will become apart of their electronic portfolios, as LaGuardia advances with a project now in its pilot phase. The electronic student portfolio, or ePortfolio, is a Web-based presentation of student work, created by the student. The ePortfolio can include research papers and essays, as well as projects that incorporate images, audio, and video. It asks students to analyze the meaning of their work, to reflect on it as a demonstration of their learning. In addition, it offers the opportunity for students to supplement course work with sections on personal interests, family, culture, and career hopes and dreams.

Linking pedagogy, technology, and assessment, the ePortfolio initiative is an ambitious one for LaGuardia. A small but growing number of colleges nationwide have begun to explore the use of ePortfolios. Most of the schools experimenting in this area, however, are small, liberal arts colleges serving more traditional students. LaGuardia may be the first large, urban community college to institute a significant ePortfolio project.

Building on classes and projects such as "Going Places," the ePortfolio may also provide a unique way for scholars and observers to better understand the changes taking place in 21st-century America. At the same time, the ePortfolio project offers LaGuardia students a chance to build their technology and communication skills, and learn new ways to tell their own stories. In concert with Digital Storytelling and other such projects, it offers students an opportunity to become the authors of the Web, to bridge the digital divide, and to make visible the stories that have been too invisible for too long.

BRIDGING THE GENOMICS DIVIDE

In a time of profound interdependence and amazing technological developments, one could imagine a better quality of life for the majority of the world's people. And yet, growing gaps exist between rich and poor, between peoples of the North and the South. We are now on the verge of a new divide. With the release of The Report of the Advisory Committee on Health Research on Genomics and World Health by the World Health Organization, attention will turn to growing inequities in the distribution of benefits from genome-related biotechnologies.

An appropriate response by the world community governments, citizens, and experts from industry and academia-would be to foster global dialogue and provide a forum for shaping the necessary governance framework through a commission on genomics and global health. Technology is a powerful tool for development. The United Nations Development Programme's Human Development

Report 2001: Making New Technologies Work for Human Development makes the case that technologies present boundless opportunities for those who create them but often end up shaping a world of inequity.

With the introduction of information technologies, our vocabularies expanded to include the concept of a digital divide. Similarly, advances in agricultural biotechnology, with the promise to the developing world of increased crop yields, additional nutritional properties, and solutions to pest control and drought, were subject to the creation of a biosafety regime designed by the North. The next wave of technology-genome-related biotechnologies in health does not has to follow that pattern. There are stark disparities in health around the globe. In industrialized countries like Norway and Australia, life expectancy is around eighty years and rising.

In sub-Saharan Africa, it is forty years and falling, largely as a result of HIV/AIDS. Many in the developing world die of "pedestrian" (malaria, tuberculosis, pneumonia. but persistently devastating infectious diseases. A coming epidemic of non communicable disease will produce a "double burden" on developing countries. The North has neglected decisive action to combat these diseases, which are now backyard menaces as the potential for pathogens to cross borders increases and changes of climate create new habitats for disease agents. This mutual destiny could be strongly influenced by the emergence of the science of genomics.

Genomics is a disruptive technology with the potential to widen or ameliorate these inequities in global health. Will we harness genomics to improve global health? Will our priority be to invest in designer pharmaco-genomics or to sequence the genome of the malaria parasite to discover new classes of drugs and develop an effective vaccine? Simply put, genomics is the study of the entire genetic material of an organism. In recent decades, new analytical tools and advances in information technology have allowed scientists to map and sequence massive amounts of genetic information and to better understand gene interactions.

The first draft of the sequence of the human genome was published in 2001, an event that raised enormous hopes. These developments hold great promise to improve the prevention, identification, and treatment of some of the major diseases affecting humankind, including HIV, malaria, and tuberculosis. Already there are examples of successful application of these technologies to health problems in developing countries. For example, using genome-related biotechnologies, health workers can diagnose infectious diseases like dengue fever more rapidly and less expensively than using current techniques.

It is known that minor genetic variations between people can influence their responsiveness to certain drug treatments, such as HIV drugs; therefore, tailoring drugs to the specific characteristics of individuals or communities can improve health and cost effectiveness. Yet health benefits, with their accompanying economic benefits, are not guaranteed. In response to other technological developments, the industrialized world has registered a range of public reaction from incredible hope to irrational fear often resulting in industry frustration and paralysis in the development of public policy. Real and perceived risks should be taken seriously.

However, one of the greatest risks would be to not seize the opportunity genomics provide to improve the health of people in developing countries, where there is limited human and institutional capacity to research local problems and use the scientific knowledge produced elsewhere. So far, health research is disproportionately directed to the developed world, leading to the so-called 10/90 gap-10 per cent of the world's population accounts for 90 per cent of research expenditure dedicated to health.

If the vision of optimizing global health benefits and minimizing the risks of advances in genomics/biotechnology is to be realized, several conditions will have to be met, decisively and urgently.

Research should focus on identifying promising biotechnologies and exploring the barriers to applying genomics knowledge in developing countries. Financial investment models that direct resources to undercapitalized genome-related biotechnologies, providing both a social and economic return on investment, should be created. The capacity of developing countries to develop the policies, institutions, and infrastructure scientific, legal, and financial to manage the risks of genome-related biotechnologies and participate effectively in international negotiations must be enhanced.

Perhaps of greatest importance is the need for informed dialogue that will lead to effective and accepted public policy. Governments, industries, and citizens in both developed and developing countries will encounter numerous ethical issues as genome-related biotechnologies are exploited.

Can these technologies be used responsibly? What should be the appropriate balance between private and public sector interests? What health needs should be given priority? How can capacity to develop an appropriate regulatory regime be built in developing countries? What policies and measures are needed to transfer and accumulate technologies to constituencies of greatest need? And perhaps the most pressing question of all: How can we ensure that the revolution in health genomics will benefit people in developing countries?

These are complex questions. The science underpinning the debate is often uncertain. Technologies are developing rapidly. Lack of understanding is a shaky foundation for effective public policy. Most important, if we are to avoid yet another source of world distrust and strife, the central question of equity in harnessing genomics deserves our best thinking. The concept of global public goods may be helpful in identifying ways to use genomics knowledge to improve global health.

The issue of intellectual property protection needs to be reexamined to find innovative ways of ensuring adequate returns to investors while increasing the likelihood that useful new technologies will be available to those in need. The patent system was designed to create incentives for innovation, not to ensure equity of access. Thus, there is a need to ensure the availability of identified global public goods through different mechanisms. There are recent signs that the rigidity and tenacity of intellectual property protection is being eroded.

The World Trade Organization discussions in Doha, Qatar, in 2001 clarified the rights of governments to invoke an emergency that would allow them to bypass intellectual property protection for drugs that are needed to save lives. Differential pricing for drugs is now gaining international support. A global dialogue that would raise awareness, perhaps build consensus, and set the agenda for action is essential. This public policy issue is not limited to an individual country or culture. It is not so much about scientific fact as about society's understanding, acceptance, and management of risk.

This is the beginning of another technological revolution with inevitable social, economic, and political changes. We would all benefit from putting the issues in context and exploring together possible approaches to their management rather than denying those with limited knowledge a voice. This interconnected world requires creative institutional arrangements that leave no one behind. There is an opportunity to put the politics of polarization aside and be architects of a participatory process worthy of the importance of the issue.

Significant public policy issues require a process of awareness, understanding, and informed debate if consensus is to be built on the appropriate and acceptable shape of decisions. In Canada, for more than 100 years, formal and informal commissions of inquiry have addressed subjects as diverse as bilingualism and biculturalism, unemployment insurance, the status of women, the economic union and development prospects, and, more recently, reproductive technologies.

Similarly, governments have developed numerous mechanisms to provide exposure to certain issues, undertake research, elicit opinion, and develop recommendations for action. Since 1990, the UN has convened over a dozen global ad hoc conferences and heads of state summits on different thematic areas, each with its own complex preparatory process. Governments and international organizations have used high-level panels, task forces, and other multistakeholder processes. They have also sponsored high-profile commissions with varying degrees of independence.

Although these mechanisms have succeeded in raising awareness of issues, they have all too often resulted in negotiated documents of principle, rather than agreed targets and schedules for action and means of ensuring compliance. Commissions have served to promote better decisions by providing a forum for broader input and the integration of diverse points of view and important expertise. They can catalyze meaningful political change supported by a public consensus.

The best are able to provide an environment in which trust and confidence are built and where committed participants come to "own" the process and the product and increase the likelihood of successful implementation of the results of the commission's work. They create "political space" for those who are absent from or are underrepresented in the policymaking process.

The genesis, mandate, approach, and institutional structure underlying models of public policy dialogue, such as the Brundtland World Commission on Environment and Development, the more recent Digital Opportunity Task Force of the G8 heads of state, and the International Campaign to Ban Landmines, differ significantly. From documentation, discussion, and direct experience, it is possible to make some observations about strategic factors that influenced the course of the initiative. Each initiative took on a life of its own and was shaped by the particular circumstances of its establishment. Nonetheless, lessons can be learned about critical decisions regarding the establishment and functioning of these mechanisms.

Key prerequisites include an "incubation period" involving extensive preliminary consultations and preparations; a focused and legitimate mandate; visionary leadership; a coherent strategy and inclusive approach; and adequately resourced and well-managed operations. In the interest of the credibility, legitimacy, and ultimate success of the exercise, it would be worth taking time now to consult extensively.

The following are examples of critical questions to be explored: Is a commission on genomics and global health the right approach for such a complex issue? Can a clear definition of scope and mandate be articulated? Could a commission function with enough urgency to provide real value to policymakers given the pace of technological developments? Is it imperative that the legitimacy of the commission be derived from association with the UN or with other forums such as the G8 or the G-20? If so, can one ensure enough flexibility to embrace learnings about transparency, inclusivity, and accountability from recent multistakeholder initiatives? Are there champions for such a dialogue within government, industry, and civil society willing to provide both leadership and funding?

A commission on genomics and global health can benefit from the lessons of its predecessors to avoid a superficial discussion that results in agreements at the lowest common denominator and to ensure that there is a bias for action. It could find ways to ensure the production and availability of global public goods related to genomics, especially in developing countries. It could transcend and go beyond where previous commissions have gone, putting people at the center of one of society's most critical debates through an open, transparent, and inclusive process.

There can be no doubt about the challenge before us: building consensus and mobilizing action to reduce global inequities in health. Yet realizing the full potential of emerging technologies in genomics and biotechnology raises numerous ethical and practical questions and suggests the need for a much better understanding of the risks and benefits. Furthermore, it demands the most creative thinking and experimentation with new models for financing, transferring technology, and building capacity in the developing World.

9

The Female Future and New Subjectivities

The assumption underpinning the third wave of optimism was that the process of computing may fundamentally challenge the common-sense universe that perceives male and female bodies differently, and via this challenge precipitate a genderless future. The suggestion is that computing may disembody and dislocate us socially and psychologically so that we may understand our relationship to our own body in a new way, one that does not recognise the limitations physicality imposes upon us.

It is also suggested that we may begin to see others very differently, may break with the historical connections we have made between perceived communication or behaviour, and the physical embodiment of the communicator or actor. The computer is thought to provoke modern consciousness into these novel ways of thinking about itself through a variety of means. It provides a screen upon which we can project images of ourselves, through which we can renegotiate 'old boundaries' between nature and culture, reason and emotion, mind and body, animate and inanimate, active and passive, self and other, and through which we can rethink the parameters of our potentialities and limitations in the process.

The computer therefore causes us to question the status quo and the fixity of human nature and becomes the foundation of 'new cultural forms'. As well as this indirect manner of provoking conceptual change, the computer is also assumed by advocates of this wave to more directly provoke transformations in consciousness. It is suggested that computer use and computer-mediated communication actively produce a new form of subjectivity, one that is 'decentred, dispersed and multiplied in continuous instability', and one to which the physical, biological body and the specifics of any space-time location cease to present limitations.

Therefore, in our thinking about us and our interactions with others, neither the body, nor the power relations with its specific historical context frames it within should continue to be prime determinants. All social inequalities which are shaped and signified by the body including gender inequalities are consequently anticipated to become redundant, anachronistic and eventually non-existent. With increasing computer use, we will engage with 'unnatural' identities and simulated truths, and in the process progress to the next phase of human development: the cyborg - the human-machine hybrid, a 'creature in a post-gender world'.

If this claim is legitimate, then computing should go some way to transforming the established gender system, and, as part of this, should reduce the obstacles which have traditionally blocked female entry into computer work. There are three inter-related claims to explore here: first, whether the computer as a projective medium has precipitated changes in the way we think about our natures, our bodies, our capabilities and our limitations, and whether these changes have any significant impact on our sense of gender identity. Secondly, whether or not the process of computing - and here are included computing activities of all kinds: computer-mediated communication such as engagement in fantasy games, programming, as well as general interacting with the computer such as internet surfing - can disembody and dislocate social consciousness generally, and genderconsciousness specifically, whilst it occurs.

Thirdly, whether it can do these things in a way that has an enduring effect on an individual or a group. Although exploring these specific claims constituted a secondary task within the research that forms the basis of this book, the data collected nevertheless provided some significant findings which have both a direct and indirect bearing on them. These findings and their relevance will be discussed below and in the conclusion.

THE COMPUTER AS PROJECTIVE MEDIUM

It is first worth noting those elements of the data that most clearly resonated with the optimistic claims. There was some suggestion, for instance, that individuals were indeed utilising the phenomenon of the computer as a key part of their ongoing thinking about human nature and consciousness, especially in relation to that of machines:

Machines will think. Human beings are purely physical systems. We can already mimic various parts, so why not all of it? Humans are just sophisticated pieces of hardware. Why can't computers cry? Our resistance to the idea is tied up with religion and ideas of the soul... computers will undoubtedly be able to emote one day, so where is the difference? I think thinking is, by definition, a human activity but I don't believe biology has something special about it. In principle there is no reason why computers can't simulate most of human behaviour, but they probably won't ever in practice because you can't allow for the chaotic elements.

However, as these quotations imply, this thinking seemed to operate at a fairly abstracted level and there was no overall coherence of opinion regarding the precise significance of intelligent machines for our selfunderstanding. For some, engagement with computers highlighted the closeness between humans and machines, and prompted them to contest the power of biology to determine thought and action. For others, it merely served to sharpen their sense of themselves as animals; unique animals maybe, but animals all the same. Furthermore, there was no sense in which either position could be neatly allied to any beliefs, including any politically inspired beliefs, in the fixity of human behaviour.

More specifically, there was no correlation between these reflections and any meditations on the question of whether or not the gendered body had any essential and unchangeable role in determining gendered behaviour. It was not therefore impossible for individuals to subscribe to a belief that humans were closer to machines than animals in that they were essentially reprogrammable rather than fixed in terms of their natures, and to simultaneously maintain that 'men and women have fundamentally different hardware, and I'm sceptical about whether it's either possible or desirable for that fact to change'.

What is notable is that there was little in the way of gender variance to observe here. Although all of those in the category who preferred to emphasise the closeness between humans and computers were men, the majority of mens' experiences with computers, as well as that of all of the women, sharpened their sense of themselves as unique animals rather than their sense that these machines were their closest cousins.

This, despite an easily understandable motivation amongst the women to more generally de-emphasises their relationship to their 'natural' or animalistic origins. What was also of interest was that the deliberations on this issue never seemed to take place in a manner that was related directly, on any explicit level at least, to an individual's sense of self-identity. These were abstract ideas which, although not infrequent conversation pieces, remained wholly removed from more personal and immediate discussions about the self. There was, therefore, little overt contradiction involved in women's conceptual and emotional subscription to a natural over a mechanical lineage and their insistence that they were not limited by any aspect of their physical make-ups.

THE COMPUTER AS SOCIAL TRANSFORMER

In terms of the more directly transformative effects of computer activity, there was some evidence which provided tentative support for the beliefs underpinning the third wave of optimism. There were, for instance, suggestions that intensive man-machine communication and computer use led to some experience of spatial and temporal disruption. Descriptions of 'getting lost' and of 'forgetting the time' were not unusual by any means, and these were sometimes explicitly linked to a sense of identity disturbance: individuals spoke specifically of 'forgetting' or 'losing' themselves in computer activity.

Significantly, however, these symptoms were not seen as qualitatively different from those experienced in other activities; the most that was claimed was that computing provided a more potent example of the mesmerising effects of other pursuits to which it was likened: building crystal radios, completing complex crosswords, etc. Where this aspect of computer activity was in evidence, it was both experienced and valued to a far greater extent by men than by women. Men were attracted to the disruptive powers of the computer, which they likened to play, where the majority of women were neutral on this issue or actively disregarded it.

It is important to note, however, that even here the effects of the computer's disruptive power seemed very limited in scope. Although they could mean someone interacting with the machine into the night without realising the time, there was no evidence that it involved any more persistent disturbance of identity, including gender identity, beyond the normal impact which many intensive and distracting activities may have. On the contrary, as the bulk of the evidence reviewed here suggests, it can be argued that the fact of men being stimulated by this aspect of computing was a key ingredient in the reproduction and consolidation of themselves as masculine men, and as superior computer scientists by dint of this.

Unsurprisingly, therefore, there was no evidence that the spatiotemporal disturbances that occurred as a result of man-machine communication went on to disrupt an individual's sense of place or power in the world - in their social consciousness. Indeed, barring those particular and partial dislocations which occurred during the process of the computing activity itself, no further disturbances were reported or evident during the entire research period. However, disruptions that occurred as a result of computer-mediated communication between humans deserve further consideration here; they provide an interesting and suggestive data framework within which the claim that inter-computational identity confusion can precipitate lasting forms of identity disturbance can be more concretely explored.

Moments of identity confusion, some of which led to role dislocation and behaviour which ran against the grain of established social hierarchies, occurred as a direct result of the use of computer-mediated communication amongst the unit's members. The use of inter- and intra - office email is a good example in this regard. Most employees were conscious of the propensity of this medium to increase the likelihood of individuals breaking out of their circumscribed social roles in a manner which was rarely seen in the context of other communications media.

Often, subjects directly echoed the views of those commentators cited and suggested that email had the capacity to be 'a good leveller'. For instance, when the collective goal was to encourage less senior individuals to speak their mind with a greater degree of assurance and confidence than their position in the organisation would normally dictate, email was seen as the best medium to use:

When we have big work or organisational debates, it often takes place over the email. It all goes over the email and nobody talks to each other about it much outside of that really, and it's almost like different rules apply. You can say things you wouldn't say face-to-face, and that's the point of setting it up that way.

Email's capacity to encourage the unit's members to express themselves in a manner which was at odds with their extra-computational roles was not, however, seen as unproblematic:

Email doesn't help conflict levels. Email is a terrible raiser of inter-office fighting ... nobody... likes to call somebody to their face too often, or if they do they can cool down before they go back and apologise... or you can go to a memo. If you write a memo, of course then it gets really serious because it's all in writing. But with email it's all a bit in the middle. And you can go back to your desk, fume away, drop a note, and a circulation list as well, an 'I'll fix him' circulation list. Press the button and then the whole world knows. And then the person at the other end thinks 'God... everyone else has seen this now' so back goes another one. We haven't really caught up socially or mentally with this.

The origin of this conflict seemed to lie in the rather equivocal responses which members of the organisation had towards the possibility of escaping the restrictions imposed by both their achieved and ascribed social roles; as well as to the possibility that others would do the same. Whilst individuals often seemed to welcome the opportunity to push back the restrictions imposed on them, they were far less enthusiastic about the possibility of others doing the same. This was especially the case if the others in question were deemed by them to be either organisationally or socially inferior. Indeed, in the event of this situation obtaining, they would often be prompted to retrench to the signifying power of bodybound identities, and the status they conferred in 'Real Life'.

And, although women more positively embraced the idea of losing the ascribed status that attached to being female, they were sceptical about the extent to which this could effectively happen in practice. Furthermore, they were no better than their male counterparts at tolerating the suspension either of information about ascribed status, or of rules structuring relations between them. The body-bound bases of these ranks were rarely far from conscious thought when individuals were in the process of deciphering the exact meaning and tenor of a communication:

In other words, computer-mediated utterances, like face-to-face ones, were routinely understood in a manner which referred them back to those social locations of the individuals which obtained outside the framework of the computer, social locations which were determined by both specific organisational and generic status positions, and the key signifier of which was the physical body.

Male bodies continued to signify something different from female bodies, old different from young, and, as well as ascribed status, achieved status such as that based on proven merit or qualifications was also signalled by the individual, embodied persona. Disembodied utterances could not be said to exist in anything other than a partial and temporary way. The fact that communication was computermediated provided at most only fleeting respite from the body-based, rule-bound nature of everyday social encounters, and certainly no lasting disruption to the established power-differentials between different members of organisational and social groupings.

It should be noted, however, that these conclusions pertain to cases where identification of the real-life, body-bound identity is ultimately nearly always possible. To more fairly evaluate the claims made by commentators, we need to consider those cases of computer-mediated communication where physical identification is not so easily made, and where the disjunction between words and their originating source is difficult to bridge. Is there more evidence in these cases for the kind of identity disruption predicted? If so, what effect, if any, does this have on the existing binary gender system?

In this study, even in those cases of computer activity where there is clearly more latitude for identity disruption, exploration and play in the absence of the body, such as games and online chat, responses to these conditions shared broadly similar characteristics to those prompted by email. There are several points to make here. The first is that, although the idea of engaging in totally disembodied communication was appealing to many subjects, the notion of others availing themselves of the same opportunity was not viewed with equal enthusiasm. Individuals were happy enough about one-off online encounters with co-communicators of unknown age, gender, rank etc., but became increasingly unhappy with this scenario if contact was repeated.

The process of establishing a relationship or getting to know someone seemed to automatically involve the desire to 'authenticate' or identify who they were by reference to very traditional criteria. They expressed negative feelings if they felt they had been 'duped' into thinking a co-communicator was, by these traditional criteria, something other than what they had presented themselves as being. This was especially the case where gender-switching was involved: 'Whatever the situation, if someone changes genders on you I don't think you can ever feel good about it'.

It was also commonplace to express amusement at the idea of someone else being duped in this way. Stories of individuals developing emotions, however tentative, for co-communicators presenting as one gender but originating as another, were a telling source of entertainment. The reactions of members of the unit to one, perhaps apocryphal story that was in circulation during the research period also illustrating the importance of the part played by the physical body in contextualising online communication. Via the email connection between parts of the organisation situated in the US and the UK came an account of a series of online encounters between President Clinton and a particular US citizen.

The President, so the story went, had established a home page at the White House through which anyone with internet access in the US could pose questions that he would personally answer. The point of the tale was that Clinton had been 'caught out' insofar as one of his main interlocutors, and someone with whom he had engaged in political debate of some sophistication, was eventually revealed to be a six-year-old boy. Within the unit, the story was instantly hailed as an illustrative example of the claim that computermediated communication was indeed the social leveller which many claimed it was.

However, following a certain amount of discussion, this initial reaction was replaced by a quieter acknowledgement that the whole reason this event, whether fictitious or not, gained the currency it did was precisely because of the feeling people had that the President had been 'fooled' into treating an online persona with a degree of respect not normally accorded to them. This fact had only come to light once the physical embodiment of the President's correspondent emerged to contextualise his utterances; utterances which were subsequently deemed to be unworthy of the level of attention they had initially received in the disembodied context of cyberspace.

In other words, despite this context's suspension of established social rules, neither the ascribed nor the achieved status of either the President or his co-communicator was changed in any significant manner or on any permanent basis. In connection with this, it is important to note that although, as Rheingold suggests, cyberspace may always lend itself to obfuscation, both online chat and email communication are likely in the future to become less disembodied, and less open to identity switching, with the predicted advent of sophisticated video-conferencing technology into these arenas.

FANTASY, FICTION AND 'REAL LIFE'

Separate consideration, however, needs to be given to the fantasy/game environment, where identity-play is both rife and expected, and where video-conferencing facilities are unlikely ever to be required or desired. Individuals seemed to understand the contact it was possible to make in these arenas as something very different from any other kind of communication. Interacting in these environments was deemed to involve a relatively self-conscious attempt to escape rules usually relied upon to structure social intercourse, rather than a catalysing or liminal moment in which the essence of the 'real', or the relationship between the body and identity, was seriously called into question: 'It's like going out and getting drunk.

You can get outside of yourself for a few hours and that's a form of relaxation. It makes a complete change from everything and I find it relaxing'. The sentiments expressed here lead neatly onto another, closely related point: whilst those individuals who so desired were happy to indulge in some disembodied interaction of their own, sometimes even masquerading as a different self, there was still no evidence that this had any general or lasting effect on their everyday sense of identity, including their gendered identity:

Furthermore, individuals did not report any changes in their beliefs about gender divisions, or about their own gender role, which were related to participating in these activities; and their colleagues failed to notice any such changes. Indeed, to echo what has been said earlier, the only significant observation which could be made was that those employees who had pursued these activities at some point in their lives were almost uniformly male and nearly always the kind of men whose engagement with computers seemed to be bound up precisely with the consolidation of themselves as conforming to a specific model of modern masculinity: 'There's a type. One used to see them at university. It's a particular type of man, almost the train spotter type. There isn't that much time to do things like that here, but you can still see the type'.

These conclusions find resonance in other empirically based analyses of computer-mediated communication contexts where disembodied communication takes place, including those cases where traditional identification of co-communicators is difficult. Much of the available evidence concurs with the finding here that there are important limitations to any noticeable process of identity disruption. It suggests that whilst some individuals seem comfortable and equipped to cope with the idea that 'normal rules' are suspended when disembodied communication occurs, this seems only to be the case where the context is clearly one of a game or fantasy.

Even then, some disquiet that others are equally free to masquerade as someone other than the person their originating identity designates is commonplace. Again, gender identification seems to be an especially sensitive issue. There are, for instance, examples of individuals revelling in the experience of duping others into believing that the presentation of a fictitious persona reflects an originating one. It is evident that people may want to dissemble for a whole variety of motives - from the wish to explore some hidden or repressed aspect of their own psychological make-up through to desire for financial remuneration. Rheingold cites some illustrative cases.

Amongst them is the young French male sex-chat worker who is paid by Minitel to masquerade as a woman for men subscribing to the service, and who is 'cynically gleeful about his performance... keeping up five conversations with credulous men preventing them from guessing the duplicity as long as possible... "the fool still believes I'm a woman!'". We also hear of 'Sue', a keen and admired MuDder (Multiuser Dungeon or Domain user). Although she seduced a series of male co-players across the internet, even to the point of eliciting a proposal of marriage from one, she was eventually revealed to be a married man with a history of fraudulent behaviour.

When both of these cases were 'unmasked' the response was far from positive. In the Minitel example, the revelation that 'false persons' were paid to keep online users subscribing led to a significant decline in chat service revenues. Sue's unmasking similarly resulted in understandable embarrassment and anger. Significantly, however, these negative responses were redoubled in a third case which Rheingold discusses: that of 'Joan'. Joan presented in a nonfantasy, non-game environment as a young New York neuropsychologist who, having been 'disfigured, crippled, and left mute' by a drunk driver, was guided towards a computer, a modem and a subscription to CompuServe where she 'instantly blossomed'.

Subsequently she became a source 'of wit and warmth' to hundreds of people, forging intimate connections with them, offering advice and consolation, especially to disabled women: 'She changed people's lives'. However, the revelation that Joan's 'Real Life' identity was that of Alex, a male, able-bodied psychiatrist engaging in some private study of the nature of female relationships, sent shock waves of betrayal through the cyberspace community.

There is an important general lesson to be drawn if we reflect on this evidence and one which constitutes a serious assault on the claims underpinning the third wave of optimism. Many people who engage with ICTs in this manner continue to mirror the broad social concerns and behaviour of those who do not, and insofar as this is the case, they seem no closer to operating within a genderless universe than anyone else. It is significant, for example that they continue to function with active distinctions between deception and 'truth', between games and serious communication, and between the online universe and 'Real Life'. Furthermore, the experience of being deceived continues to involve the denial of traditional categories of identification, and continues to be considered an uncomfortable one.

It is worth noting here that much of the hyperbole surrounding the discussions about the potential for identity disturbance within this medium may be a function of the fact that a particular group of those most intensely involved in computer-mediated communication, especially the game environment, has become the most common empirical resource of commentators in the field: adolescents, and especially male adolescents. This group have often been considered the 'natural' constituents of cyberspace, but they have also long been identified by sociologists and psychologists as distinctive in some important senses.

One such sense is a preoccupation with elements of fluidity and confusion which characterise their private and public sense of self, especially those aspects which impact on issues of gender, sexuality and power. However, it would seem to be a mistake to build expectations of generalised and radical social change on the basis of this specific community's enthusiastic embrace of the identity-disturbing aspects of cyberspace. It is just as likely that the broader computer-using population will remain wedded to the maintenance of a clear sense of 'authentic' relationships, ones which can be 'trusted', and that these will continue to be those where there is an assumed correlation between the physical body in the domain of 'Real Life' and its representation in the domain of cyberspace.

In support of this conclusion is the fact that, in recent years, explicit rules have begun to emerge to regulate the behaviour of those individuals who seek to transgress the tacit, shared sense of appropriate action within and across the two domains. The creation of social life usually involves a build-up of basically utilitarian rules which inhibit our own desires (which may conflict with another's interests), but also inhibit another's desires (which may in turn conflict with interests closer to home).

This framework creates a protective trade-off that compensates for the loss of total freedom, and it has been imported into cyberspace where the potential for identity-switching is becoming increasingly subject to the kind of regulatory rules which shape other areas of social life. Both subtle and hard-line social sanctions, for instance, have emerged to inhibit the 'modem butterfly' practice of online gender deception, and a face-saving default assumption that female-presenting characters are male unless proven otherwise is not uncommon.

Even in dedicated 'play' contexts, where all participants have agreed to a suspension of real-life rules, game-rules have emerged which are designed to maintain some sense of stability and trust within and between presenting identities. This form of netiquette dictates, for example, that individuals should not masquerade under another's created persona, even if this is an entirely fictitious one, and that those who do risk censure. Indeed, some of the empirical studies of the online landscape indicate that rather than the physical body being undermined in this domain, and rather than the established script of gender being contested and rewritten, an augmentation of these phenomena may even be occurring.

Susan Herring's detailed analysis of the discourse of computer-mediated communication suggests that it takes place within an archetypally maledominated and male-oriented framework. This is the case despite the quantitative increase in female participation in games and online discussion forums, where there are ample opportunities for female participation and gender-switching. It has been claimed that in the absence of the body as identifier, men seize the opportunity to express their most negative feelings about women and femininity as 'the other'.

For women, entering the online environment has consequently been likened to 'walking downs a city street in a short skirt', as female-presenting personas are subjected to an intensification of some of the worst excesses of male-to-female behaviour: 'insults, harassment, gratuitous nastiness and condescension'. Furthermore, it would seem that, for women as much as men, the standard expectations of masculinity and femininity remain firmly attached to projected identities in cyberspace, as women are not immune to the lure of parodic masculine behaviour towards female-presenting characters when presenting as men. In this context, those who claim far larger proportions of female online users than is commonly accepted cannot automatically presume that quantitative changes will precipitate any qualitative modifications in the culture of cyberspace.

In sum, it is the projected identity that the gendered behaviour follows, and the behaviour of those presenting as men and those presenting as women complies with the established gender categories very rigidly; arguably more rigidly than they do off-line. The fact that individuals can effectively masquerade as the opposite gender to their originating one does not herald the breakdown of real-life gender patterns. Rather, it seems to underscore their resilience. Indeed, it has been justifiably claimed that the online environment provides them with the opportunity to reproduce prototypes of each gender, expressed, significantly, as physical ideals:

In physical reality, it's not so easy to become the he-man or the Barbie ...the crystallisation of notions of masculinity and femininity. However, in a virtual world, stereotypical ideas about gender and sexuality can simply be brought to bear without the inevitable contingencies and imperfections that plague the act of physically embodying a gender identity. What this discussion points to is the limitation of the computer's propensity to precipitate fundamental changes to human consciousness, including gender consciousness, and to the over-arching social order that such consciousness is a determination of. For, as well as there being little evidence of individuals contesting established gender scripts whilst online, there is also no evidence that online behaviour, whatever its character, affects real-life gendered conduct.

The claim that human-machine interaction produces a creative disjunction between our established sense of identity and a multifarious online self finds little support here. Similarly, the claim that the possibilities for deception and identity-play have become so prevalent with computer-mediated communication that they will erase the boundaries between cyberspace and Real Life, between the male body and the female body, cannot easily be sustained. Engagement with ICTs may indeed create a new dimension to social life, but there seems to be little or no basis as yet for believing that this will not become colonised by the rules of other, extra-computational dimensions.

What does seem clear is that despite an undoubted willingness to explore the potential for identity disruption and gender-bending on the part of many who are enthusiastic about this technology, there is clearly a countervailing reluctance, or inability, to relinquish the established social concepts and cues that guide us meaningfully through the daily morass of action and interaction. This framework of rules is organised around several key axes, a major one of which is the physical body. In a fundamental sense, the body remains the corporeal basis for reproducing ourselves as single-selves and as single gendered.

Modern servicing provision is based on the production and exchange of intangibles - knowledge, information, emotional support, co-operation and facilitation. The increasing centrality of these 'products' has put social labour of a variety of kinds more firmly on the map. Starting with Daniel Bell's claim in The Coming of Post-Industrial Society that the post-war growth of the service sector meant that 'communication' and 'encounter' has become the most salient relationship in the overall organisation of work, the assertion that the fastest-growing occupational group centres on workers who require 'interpersonal' skills to help them deal with people, as opposed to 'mechanical' skills which help them interact with objects, has become increasingly commonplace.

Service sector workers, perhaps represented most effectively by those in the burgeoning tourist industry, and knowledge workers, including doctors, lawyers, market analysts, educators, counsellors and administrators, are increasingly expected to deploy social and communication skills that conform to established general rules, regulations and values. These rules derive from the self-same push to further professionalise labour processes according to standards imposed by the general shift to a servicing ethos.

Softech's requirement for social skills to be included in the occupational profile of its optimal worker is therefore not only entirely in step with changes taking place within the computing industry at large but also with the general developmental direction of the UK and the US occupational markets. The claim that we are entering a 'female' era and that women should accordingly celebrate, rather than seek to erase, both their femininity and the socialisation path which produced it, has also gained in prominence within occupations outside of the computer industry.

Indeed, wherever social labour has been recognised as growing in importance, there has usually been a widespread optimistic anticipation that women are currently, and will continue to be, best placed to capitalise on this development. It is suggested that it is precisely those aspects of social and emotional labour with which women have become historically associated that are placed at the heart of the sectoral shifts shaping modern economies. Conversely, it is precisely those aspects of social labour associated with men which are eschewed by the emergent occupational market.

The prevailing modern organisational ethos dovetails with qualities 'which women's socialisation has emphasised'. Femininity as it has been generally constructed, and women's ability to think and act relationally, as opposed to men's preponderance to compete, dominate and aggress, is what allegedly guarantees women's future success. A continued under-evaluation of their working style, and the skills which underpin it, would, it is claimed, run too obviously against the grain of business wisdom to be a serious threat to this opportunity.

As this occupational shift becomes established, and as social skills grow in their ability to unlock the control of other valuable resources, women, according to this perspective, should expect to redress some fundamental gender imbalances which have characterised fiestern cultures to date. Harland

Cleveland, for instance, has argued that the primacy of information as a commodity in the future means that women will have the 'cultural edge' in labour markets, and that this in turn may undermine the hierarchical systems that keep two billion people in relative poverty, and one-third of them in absolute poverty. It may upset - in some societies, including ours, is already upsetting - the systems that historically relegated the female of the species to second-class citizenship.

The question is, does any of the evidence provided by this particular empirical study give pause to these more general predictions that the future will be female? The first point to make in answering this question is that the maintenance of any predicted advantage gained by female developers by the shift to a hybrid skill profile would necessitate either the neutral recognition of women's skills, or recognition of them in terms of the same set of criteria as their male counterparts. This is not to automatically assume that, if this situation obtained, all the women in the unit would have rightfully found themselves managing their lesser-skilled male colleagues.

It is therefore not claimed here that the women in the unit all possessed good social skills which were unfairly overlooked, or that the men all possessed minimal social skills, but found themselves praised for them anyway. To broaden this point out, it is also not claimed that all women have better social and communication skills than all men, and certainly not that any edge which they might possess in this respect is the result of biological programming. In relation to this, the key presuppositions of those I have characterised as second-wave optimists need to be examined critically along with the veracity of their predictions.

The focus instead has been the complex nature of the processes whereby occupational skills are recognised and ascribed; and the fact that such processes privilege male workers and their competencies, regardless of the content of skills possessed by women. This is because skill assessments remain contingent on different contexts and on the socio-political interests that inform them, and more specifically, that they continue to be inextricably bound up with systems of common-sense assumptions regarding the social status of men and women.

The focus has also fallen on the fact that the biased nature of skill assessment processes has real, material effects on men and women working today. It is as a result of these processes that the women in the unit were, in abstract, explicitly recognised by their colleagues as possessing good levels of interpersonal expertise, but were rarely, if ever, the recipients of the concretised form of this recognition: rewards, respect and remuneration.

The idea that women are 'wrong' for the task in hand, not because they do not possess the necessary skills, but because they are the wrong gender, is fundamentally important here. If these principles are accepted to be even partially true, and even partially applicable to other contexts, crucial questions are begged regarding the possibility of women easily taking up fully functioning roles within fields that are defined as skilled. This obtains regardless of the kind of skills required, and regardless of which gender they have historically been associated with.

The study's findings also suggest that the general problem women face in having their skills recognised and rewarded is exacerbated in occupations which involve intellectual and/or social labour to a large degree. The heightened level of indeterminacy involved in the processes mediating the identification and recognition of such skills tends to produce judgements about the skill of an individual which are more closely bound up with judgements regarding their social status.

More specifically, the fact that the skills involved in the undertaking of social labour are so closely bound up with emotion has merely compounded the general rule underpinning the differential assessments of male and female competencies in this particular case, because, as Hochschild's work has revealed, the feelings, as well as the actions, of higher-status individuals are privileged - noted and taken seriously - as compared to those of lower status.

It is important to note in connection with this that despite the increasingly predominant role of social labour in the wider occupational market, it remains represented and articulated in relatively immature terms at the level of formal or even explicit occupational skill categories, to the extent that it is far from universally clear what this, and similar terms (emotional labour, communications work, performance work), precisely denote. These skills have yet to be subjected to the processes which make up the formal components of other skills, which produce the framework for more objective recognition and assessment: the disaggregation of competence into its discrete component parts, methodical codification, the construction of training programmes, certification, and near-universal recognition.

Consequently, the manner in which such skills are currently identified and calibrated is less systematic and more complex than it is in almost every other skill categorisation area, to the extent that terms such as 'social skills' remain comparatively empty descriptors. In the absence of easily identifiable objective indices of successful deployment of such competencies, such as sales invoices which can be directly related to an individual's social effectiveness rather their product's attractiveness, the process of identifying them remains heavily reliant upon common-sense or inadequately conceived notions formed by management or peers about what constitutes proficiency in this area.

Of course, the exact structure of social competency may never be fully articulated and explicated. Some employers have made preliminary attempts to pin it down more precisely with the use of tools such as personality tests, but there is fairly compelling evidence that these have so far proved only minimally successful for this purpose. It is necessary to acknowledge, however, that whilst difficulties undoubtedly accompany this task, these only partially explain the current lack of social skills codification. The evidence here strongly suggests that powerful sociopolitical interests also operate to maintain the existing high levels of indeterminacy.

During her twelve years at the company, the woman in question had never worked on a project that had been anything other than a huge success. It wasn't obvious what she was adding but projects always succeeded when she was around. After watching her in class for a week and talking to some of her co-workers, I came to the conclusion that she was a superb catalyst. Teams naturally gelled better when she was there.

This includes those attempts to mystify that are prompted by a desire to correct the pervading view of women as relatively unskilled and to highlight their intrinsic superiority in relation to the possession of social competencies. It is clear that in the past, as MacDonald has argued, the best way forward for many groups of women pursuing a professional status has been to emulate male tactics of social closure: to opt for the construction of a female habitus involving an often essentialist definition of themselves as the only sex which can appropriately undertake the work, and to maintain levels of indeterminacy within the work profile so that such a habitus can better take hold.

It is equally clear that the optimism of some of the feminist commentators cited here is based on the belief that this strategy remains the best one to adopt. Such a strategy is, however, ill-judged. In the current climate the danger is that pursuing it will serve the interests of the dominant group in any occupational area. What this study also highlights is that an emerging clusters of organisational features which often parallel the shift to focusing on social capital in the information community and wider occupational market, may further exacerbate the problem of female exclusion.

These include an assumption of meritocracy and the erosion of old-style hierarchies, along with the associated informality and high degree of indeterminacy in the assessment of the human resource, and, in particular, the interlinking of assessment systems with informal peer review systems. It would seem that 'progressive' organisational structures such as these, however well intentioned, require a firm foundation in progressive social and psychological relations if they are to avoid mutating into their opposite.

The general conclusion from the present study is that a cultural lag exists between some key 'progressive' developments in organisations and current levels of socio-political consciousness, and that this often renders such developments conservative rather than liberal in their effects. Had the common-sense universe within the unit genuinely reflected the explicit ethos enshrined in many of its structures and goals, these would have surely proved to be as enlightened in practice as they were designed to be in theory.

Under these circumstances, it would make sense to have a minimal formal hierarchy, an attempt to occlude the gender of the individuals employed, and a system of assessment based upon the expectation that disinterested individuals freely accorded respect where it was genuinely deserved. Even having fairly indeterminate skill descriptors would be relatively unproblematic.

However, despite the confident heralding of 'twenty-first-century' employee consciousness to match policies imagined to suit it - 'we are a twenty-first-century organisation with a twenty-first-century workforce' -, the conclusion from the evidence presented here is that no such consciousness had emerged in Softech. Systematic rules of social and occupational prejudice, and ultimately of self-replication, were more expressive of the incumbent and most powerful group's 'taste' than professionally defensible choices. They formed patterns of preferential treatment for one person or another, one gender or another, albeit largely unconsciously.

The 'progressive' features of the unit therefore ultimately failed the female workers. The official cleaving to a belief that the unit lacked many hierarchical elements found in more traditional environments, and that this was more facilitative of meritocracy, and the belief that individuals were perceived as ungendered equals, failed them because it masked the operation of powerful informal social hierarchies. It presumed a level playing field where one could not possibly exist. As one male worker put it, 'we assume, in a sense, that we are all white middleclass men, which is a little unfortunate for those of us who are not'.

This meant that complaints about discrimination could not easily be heard and, equally, special allowances for someone's difference, however justified, could not easily be made. What resulted from the lack of formal hierarchy was not, as was intended, an organisational structure which distributed power and opportunity more equally and liberated creativity, but the creation of a series of unregulated social spaces within which the most likely outcome was a default to the established cultural and social hierarchies of the pre-existing computer culture and its practices.

In sum, the findings discussed here indicate that the optimism with which many have viewed the evolving relationship between women and occupations requiring social and interpersonal skills is somewhat naive. On the basis of the present study, and its supporting literature, it is reasonable to argue for the general conclusion that until those more intangible skills and outcomes are better defined, there is little reason for believing that the 'golden opportunity' thesis will be realised. Even if such skills and outcomes were better defined, and recognition of them could consequently take place on a more disinterested basis, there is no guarantee that the situation would dramatically improve for female workers in the context of the existing gender system.

The findings discussed in relation to the third wave of optimism accord with these main conclusions, despite their different focus, and insofar as they do, they are equally possessed of a more general relevance beyond the specific phenomena of computing. In pointing to the severely limited capacity of computing to dislocate us from the gendered body and disrupt gender consciousness, they also strongly signal the fact that gender remains a primary determinant of social life, and one that is not easily subject to either radical or permanent change.

Indeed, this is the most salient point to emerge from this study and its supporting literature. The dimensions of the existing gender system mean that although it is neither a universal nor a static phenomenon, it is something which operates and is reproduced at a trans-individual and even trans-national level in terms of its key precepts. As such, and in relation to these precepts, it is modified according to a scale and a time-span the scope of which all but swamps the effects of changes at the local level, in the short term, and in relation to more local or transitory social changes, however innovative and powerful these may be.

In terms of the UK and the US, these key precepts are, firstly, that there are two gender groups - masculine and feminine - allied to the two sex categories - male and female - and our membership of one or the other is not optional; rather, it is a function of our biological sex. Secondly, that for the most part, what is deemed masculine is privileged and what is deemed feminine is under-valued and marginalised. Thirdly, that the gendered body is a primary signifier of each individual's role in the system and of the inequality that characterises it. It, and what it signifies, play a key part in helping us make sense of our world, even in cyberspace, where physical representation can be temporarily suspended, and even in organisations which claim to be 'skill-shopping not bodyshopping'.

During the three decades which have seen the computer's ascendance, these 'basic' rules of gender have been allied to a series of conceptual and practical binary structures in UK and US societies, rules which form a different stratum of the gender system and which, at any given moment, construct the differences between the masculine and the feminine. Included here are the distinctions currently drawn between the rational and the emotional, the technical and the social, and the skilled and the unskilled, all of which were indicated three decades ago and continue to be indicated now, as evidenced by this case study. Changes at this level of the gender system do occur, and more scope exists for modification than in relation to its foundational precepts, but any alteration takes place slowly and incrementally and is unlikely to produce lasting changes in the basic rules.

It is at a different level still that the gendering of individuals in daily contexts is reproduced, and here there is a comparatively large degree of flexibility. A diverse multiplicity of different gender roles exist for men and women to adopt, and individuals, or even groups, may also manifest

Bibliography

Archibald, Jacqueline et al. (eds.). *The Gender Politics of ICT*. London: Middlesex University Press, 2005.

Barbercheck, Mary et al. (eds.). *Women, Science, and Technology, 2nd edition..* New York: Routledge, 2008.

Burger, Carol J. et al. (eds.). *Reconfiguring the Firewall: Recruiting Women to Information Technology across Cultures and Continents.* Wellesley, MA: AK Peters, Ltd., 2007.

Cohoon, J. McGrath and William Aspray (eds.). *Women and Information Technology: Research on Underrepresentation.* Cambridge, MA: MIT Press, 2006

Collet, Isabelle. *L'informatique A-T-Elle Un Sexe : Hackers, Mythes Et Réalités.* France: L'Harmattan, 2006.

Casula, Clementina and Alessandro Mongili. *Donne Al Computer : Marginalità E Integrazione Nell'utilizzo Delle ICT.* Italy: CUEC, 2007

Cummings, S. J. R. et al. (eds.). *Gender and ICTs for Development: A Global Sourcebook.* Amsterdam: KIT Publishers, 2005.

Elm, Malin Sveningsson and Jenny Sundén (eds.). *Cyberfeminism in Northern Lights: Digital Media and Gender in a Nordic Context.* Newcastle-upon-Tyne, England: Cambridge Scholars Publishing, 2007.

Fox, Mary Frank et al. (eds.). *Women, Gender, and Technology.* Champaign, IL: Univ. of Illinois Press, 2006.

Gender Links and Gender and Media Southern Africa. *IT For Advocacy Manual: Making IT Work for Gender Justice.* 2005.

Guide to Promote Your Products and Services on the Internet. Miramar, FL: Heidi Richards, 2006

Gurumurthy, Anita et al. (eds.). *Gender in the Information Society: Emerging Issues.* New Delhi, India: Elsevier, 2006.

Gurumurthy, Anita. *Gender and ICTs: Overview Report.* Brighton, U.K.: Institute for Development Studies, 2004.

Haynes, Deborah J. et al. (eds.). *Gender, Race, and Information Technology.* A special issue of the journal *Frontiers: A Journal of Women's Studies.* Vol. 26, No. 1, 2005.

Huyer, Sophia and Gunnar Westholm. *Gender Indicators in Science, Engineering and Technology.* Paris: UNESCO Publishing, 2007

Kitetu, Catherine Wawasi. *Gender, Science and Technology: Perspectives from Africa.* Dakar, Senegal: CODESRIA, 2008.

Leung, Linda. *Virtual Ethnicity: Race, Resistance and the World Wide Web.* Aldershot, U.K.: Ashgate Publishing, Ltd., 2005

Mihalec, Kristina and Nevenka Sudar. *Women & Internet: Croatian Perspective.* Zagreb, Croatia: 2004.

Morgan, K. et al. (eds.). *Human Perspectives in the Internet Society: Culture, Psychology, and Gender.* Southampton, U.K.:WIT Press, 2004.

Ng, Cecilia and Swasti Mitter (eds.). *Gender in the Information Society.* A special issue (8:1) of *Gender, Technology, and Development.* New Delhi, India: Sage Publications India Pvt. Ltd., 2004.

Paasonen, Susanna. *Figures of Fantasy: Internet, Women and Cyberdiscourse.* New York: Peter Lang, 2005.

Reiche, Claudia and Verena Kuni (eds.). *Cyberfeminism: Next Protocols.* Brooklyn, New York: Autonomedia, 2004.

Rosser, Sue V. *The Science Glass Ceiling: Academic Women Scientists and the Struggle to Succeed.* New York: Routledge, 2004.

Scott-Dixon, Krista. *Doing IT: Women Working in Information Technology.* Toronto, CA: Sumach Press, 2004. .

Thomas, Sue. *Hello World: Travels in Virtuality.* York, UK: Raw Nerve Books, 2004.

Schiebinger, Londa (ed.). *Gendered Innovations in Science and Engineering.* Palo Alto, CA: Stanford University Press, 2008

Trauth, Eileen M. (ed.). *Encyclopedia of Gender and Information Technology, 2 vols.* Hershey, PA: Idea Group Reference, 2006.

Turner, Eva, ed. *Women in Computing.* Special issue of the *Journal of Information, Communication, and Ethics in Society,* vol 3, issue 4 (2005).

Wajcman, Judy. *TechnoFeminism.* Williston, VT: Blackwell Publishing, 2004.

White, Michele. *The Body and the Screen: Theories of Internet Spectatorship.* Cambridge, MA: MIT Press, 2006.

Williams, F. Mary and Carolyn J. Emerson. *Becoming Leaders: A Practical Handbook for Women in Engineering, Science, and Technology.* Reston, VA: American Society of Civil Engineers, 2008.

Women's EsCommerce Association, International. *Get More Business: The Women's eMarketing*

Zafra, Remedios. *Netianas : N(H)acer Mujer En Internet.* Spain: Lengua de Trapo, 2005.

Zorn, Isabel et al. (eds.). *Gender Designs IT: Construction and Deconstruction of Information Society Technology.* Wiesbaden, Germany: Verlag für Sozialwissenschaften, 2007.